GREAT

BRITAIN

Channel

English

CHANNEL
ISLANDS (BR.)

Calais

Boulogne-sur-Mer

Dunkerque

BELGIUM

Lille

NETHERLANDS

'EST

Cherbourg

Le Havre

Rouen

Seine

PARIS

Marne

GI

A

LUX

Metz

Strasbou

Nancy

Le Mans

Orléans

Seine

Loire

Nantes

Bay

of

Biscay

F R A N C E

Loire

JURA MTS.

SWITZER

Lake
Geneva

Mulhouse

Lyon

A
L
P
S

Rhone

Bordeaux

ITAL

Toulouse

P Y R E N E E S

SPAIN

Sète

Gulf of Lion

Nice

Marseille

Sea

Mediterranean

MAP OF FRANCE

CORSICA

An Introduction to the French Economy.

John Sheahan

Williams College

Charles E. Merrill Publishing Company
A Bell & Howell Company
Columbus, Ohio

for Yvette and Bernard

Merrill's Economic Systems Series
William P. Snavely, Editor

Standard Book Numbers: 675-09492-5 paper

675-09493-3 cloth

Library of Congress Catalog Card Number: 73-77441

Printed in the United States of America

1 2 3 4 5 6 7 8 9 10 11 12 13 14 15 — 76 75 74 73 72 71 70 69

Editor's Foreword

The Merrill Economic Systems Series has been developed to meet three clearly recognized needs. First, it is designed to provide greater flexibility and broader coverage in formal economic systems courses. To do so, the series contains a core volume and ten books covering individual countries. The core volume presents an analytical discussion, placed in historical perspective, of the major types of systems. The individual country-study volumes, written by outstanding scholars and specialists on the country, provide illustrations of the nature and operation of various systems in practice. The ten countries included in the initial series illustrate a wide range of economic systems. Those who are involved with the systems field will find it possible to choose from this extensive selection those particular country-study volumes which fit most effectively their own individual courses. As the series is expanded to include additional countries the flexibility of choice will become even greater.

The second important need which this series is designed to meet is that for collateral reading in various social science courses. Those who teach principles of economics, introductory political science, comparative government, or general social studies courses, will find excellent possibilities for assigning individual volumes for greater in-depth study of particular areas. Each book has been prepared as an entity in itself and can therefore profitably be studied either individually or as part of a more comprehensive program.

Finally, this series will provide a stimulating introduction to different economic systems for the interested reader who is concerned about this subject of major contemporary importance.

William P. Snavely

PREFACE

This review of the French economy as of the end of 1968 is in many respects more critical and less optimistic than my earlier study of French industry. This is partly because economic policy in the 1960's has been infected by inconsistencies and misdirection that have undermined some of the positive forces operating at the beginning of the decade. It is also in part a consequence of the difference in range of issues considered. The earlier book focused on industrial modernization, which has had high priority and has been relatively successful. Consideration of a wider set of goals and problems makes clear that other objectives of the society have been comparatively neglected. The French economy is still most unevenly developed. But it has one outstanding appeal as a subject of study. Policies and behavior keep changing all the time, providing fine examples of both instructive mistakes and genuine achievements.

Special thanks are due to Alain Cotta, Jan Dessau, John Hackett, Jacques Houssiaux, and Alexander Nowicki, for helpful discussions about the operation of the French economy. They bear no responsibility at all for the interpretations presented, but they made it possible to make this book more accurate and relevant than it could otherwise have been.

I would also like to express my appreciation to friends who read and commented on parts or all of various drafts. Henry Bruton, John Eriksson, Earl McFarland, Clara Park, Denise Sheahan, and Nat Weinberg contributed most useful criticisms. Judith Nichols and Paul Becher of Charles E. Merrill Publishing Company, made the process of editing and publication both efficient and unusually agreeable.

John Sheahan
Williamstown, Mass.
February, 1969

v

Contents

1 The Modern Economy and its Background   **1**

2 Agriculture   **9**
The Tradition of Protection   9
Promotion of Structural Change   11
The Common Market   15

3 Industry   **21**
Industrial Structure and Behavior   22
Government Ownership   26
Planning at the Industry Level   29
Postwar Changes in Demand and in Product Behavior   30
Concentration   33
American Investment and the Technological Race   34

4 Labor   **37**
The National Confederations   38
Negotiation Techniques and Strikes   43
Wages   46
Authority and Communication Within the Firm   50
Current Strains and the Strikes of May, 1968   53

5 Social Welfare   **57**
Family Allowances   58
Medical Benefits   60
Effects on Costs and Incentives   64
Social Investment and Education   65

6 Planning   **71**
The Early Plans: Modernization of Industry   71
The Recent Plans: Social Goals and Overall Policies   76
Democratic Control   79

7   Monetary Management and the Tax Structure   83
      The Monetary System 83
      Recent Changes in Monetary Techniques   86
      The Tax Structure   87

8   Growth and Prices   93
      Investment and Reallocation of Resources   93
      Inflation   96
      *Deflation, Unemployment, and Present Policy
        Alternatives   103*

9   Goals and Performance   107
      Personal Security   108
      Freedom of Choice   109
      Equity   110
      Access to New Opportunities   111
      Intervention and Performance   112

      Index   115

The Modern Economy
And Its Background

1

Postwar French economic policy has attempted to break away from many of the traditional characteristics of capitalism without losing freedom of choice. Economic planning, a large dose of government ownership, international agreements controlling group trade in agricultural products, a far-reaching system of social welfare, and many unorthodox combinations of regulatory and tax techniques have been used to change the ways the economy operates. At the same time, private ownership has been maintained for most of manufacturing industry and for agriculture, producers are allowed to go their own way if they choose to ignore the economic plans, and everyone remains as free as in any other western country to work where, and to the extent, he chooses. It is still essentially a capitalist system, but one guided and controlled to an unusual degree.

The main reason that planning and other techniques of more conscious direction were introduced at the start of the postwar period is that the previous performance of the economy had been exasperatingly mediocre. The prewar system had combined the defects of inequality with very little of the force for efficiency and progress associated with capitalism in many other industrial countries. Profit had been less the special reward of creative action than the stubbornly defended privilege of those who happened to own property. Business was always interested in making

1

money, but rarely in taking risks or introducing change of any kind. Government policy had supported this defensive approach, frequently blocking any sign of competitive pressure that might threaten small business, small farmers, or older ways of production. The joint effect of these preferences was to maintain a relatively stable but unprogressive economy, as well as a social climate fostering acute class conflict.

The prewar system was called capitalism, but that was in many ways an unfair label. Many of its central characteristics were much the same as those denounced by Adam Smith in the eighteenth century. They were pre-capitalistic, mixing in mercantilist notions of opposition to imports with medieval ideas of self-regulated individual markets. The French always mistrusted market forces, preferring to arrange the economy consciously. Before the war, this preference for deliberate control was used mainly to stabilize and protect; since the war, it has been intended to promote a more modern economy.

The sharper conflicts in French economic policy have not often been focused on questions of control versus reliance on competitive market solutions. They have rather been concerned with the question of whether control should be exercised by the government or instead by private groups of producers left largely to arrange markets as they chose. Sometimes the strength of the attachment to self-regulation by producers makes the medieval guild system seem very much alive. The approach is not confined to businessmen. French unionism has always had an influential current of syndicalism, favoring collective control of industries by their workers, in opposition equally to capitalism and to the state. Sugar beet growers, the guild of architects, and many other professional associations, are still allowed to fix rules of conduct, quality standards, and sometimes prices. Agricultural and industrial associations may be allowed to use private tax systems, enforceable through the courts, to collect funds from all members for such purposes as stockpiling to support prices, or even (as in textiles) to buy out producers and destroy equipment in order to reduce capacity considered to be excessive.

The concept of a protective system, in which the society or a private group maintains responsibility for the individual, and at the same time imposes constraints on his choices as to the ways in which he may earn his income, can be made to sound either highly modern or a survival of feudalism. Concern with a "just price" sounds medieval, but concern with business responsibility and "reasonable" pricing can be found in the latest issue of practically every French (or American) business journal. Grave suspicion about the moral legitimacy of profit was a major theme in French religious thinking during the many centuries in which the French took their religion extremely seriously. When it appears in left-wing statements today, it gains a force from the past that it does not have in the United States. In France, it both tends to cripple the operation of capitalism and to increase the willingness to experiment with new forms of collective action.

The protective strand is accompanied by another line of thought rooted in French history. When the society moved out of the medieval period toward the modern world, it did so for a time with great success. France was the richest and most powerful country in the world in the century preceding England's industrial revolution. Precise national accounts for the seventeenth century are hard to come by, but the economy under Colbert and other strong administrative leaders of that time seems to have been extraordinarily dynamic. This thrust did not come from reliance on private market forces, but from promotional policies of the national government. Choices on economic matters have been conditioned ever since by identification of exceptional achievement with conditions of active government leadership.

The French went some distance toward free trade and other forms of economic liberalism in the nineteenth century, but always with more reluctance than the English.[1] And history worked out to make the experience painful. Shortly after the introduction of free trade in 1860, North American and Australian exports began to drive down prices and incomes in European agriculture, and the whole world trading system entered a prolonged period of monetary deflation. France gave up on free trade and *laissez-faire* with great speed. That did not help much either. The economy did advance, but it failed to keep up with the pace of change and growth being accomplished in the rest of industrial Europe and the United States.

In 1870, France was one of the four countries which dominated the world's industrial production. Output of manufactured goods was about four-fifths as great as that of Germany, and two-fifths that of the United States. By 1913, manufacturing output was only 41 percent as high as in Germany, and 18 percent of that in the United States.[2]

One important factor bearing on this relative decline in production was that population growth was unusually low. Another was that agricultural protection eased pressures to make people move from farming into more productive urban employment. Both of these characteristics acted to restrict the growth of the labor supply available for industry, and the growth of domestic markets as well. This need not have precluded increasing sales: the whole outside world was available as a market. But

---

[1]Cf. Shepard B. Clough, *France, A History of National Economics, 1789–1939* (New York: Charles Scribner's Sons, 1939), and Charles P. Kindleberger, *Economic Growth in France and Britain, 1851–1950* (Cambridge, Mass.: Harvard University Press, 1964).

[2]Shepard B. Clough, *European Economic History* (New York: McGraw-Hill Book Company, 1968), p. 397.

exporters of manufactured goods were not notably successful, perhaps in part because the country's protectionist policies acted to hold domestic costs higher than they could have been with greater freedom to import.

The slow rate of population growth from the middle of the nineteenth century to the middle of the twentieth was one of the most striking characteristics of French society. The net reproduction rate frequently went below 1.00 (the rate necessary for the population to reproduce itself) from 1850 onward. It stayed persistently below that rate after 1900. Birth rates went down moderately for the whole period, then abruptly so in the 1930's. This behavior may have been partly caused by economic constraints. The relatively slow opening of new opportunities made it necessary for people to choose cautiously between more children or rising living standards for the family. But such economic considerations must have been only a small part of the story. Behavioral patterns in many dimensions—demographic, social, and political, as well as economic —all suggested a widespread resistance to change. The society seemed to be trying to stand still, as if afraid of the future.

The generally slow pace of the economy and the society did not make everyone unhappy. It apparently struck a chord of preferences not common in the United States: many of the country's intellectual leaders contributed to a process of rationalizing relative failure into a higher principle of success. As opposed to the materialistic pursuit of change in less mature societies, the French would show the superiority of a well-balanced, self-sufficient country, preserving the traditional virtues of the small farmer, the craftsman, and the small, family-run business. And it worked, in the sense that older ways of doing things were well protected from change.

This intellectual parallel to the Maginot Line seemed especially appealing at the beginning of the depression in 1929–30. The relatively insulated French economy managed at first to stay close to its former levels of production and employment. Exports were not nearly as important as in England, because they had never been as successfully developed; this in turn meant that their decline in the depression did not have as strong an impact on the domestic economy. The industrial sector and the urban labor force were much less important in France than in England or the United States, so overt unemployment never reached as high a proportion of the total labor force. What might have appeared to be simple failure to make progress began to look more as if it were a sensible choice in favor of stability. But it did not continue to look that way very long.

After their plunge into extremely severe unemployment from 1929 to 1932, England, the United States, and most other industrial countries began to move back up. But the French economy, somewhat as if it had a gyroscope inside to slow down the pace of reactions, slid steadily downward. By 1937–38, European industrial production as a whole had recovered to a level 11 percent above its earlier peak in 1929; in France industrial production was still 14 percent below its 1929 level. It did not get back up to the 1929 peak until 1950.[3]

Generalized frustration with an apparently helpless government led to much the same reaction as in the United States a few years earlier, a swing to the left, bringing in the Popular Front Government of Léon Blum. Blum, the head of the Socialist Party, became Premier in June, 1936. He quickly introduced major changes in legislation affecting labor and social welfare, which struck conservative French businessmen about as happily as those of the New Deal did conservatives in the United States. They ran into an immediate difficulty that had not overshadowed the early days of the New Deal. German militarism under Hitler made it clear that the possibility of war was deadly serious. The government that had been elected to carry out major social reforms had to start an immediate rearmament program. Those who regarded the legal imposition of a 40-hour work week with paid vacations as an intolerable blow to private business found it easy to denounce the reform as a fatal handicap to the defense of the country.

The conflict between social reform and the necessities of a new defense program was compounded by mediocre handling of economic recovery. The labor reforms raised costs and led to rising prices despite a high level of unemployment. The franc had to be devalued before the end of 1936. This was a logical move in the circumstances, but its invariably unfortunate connotations in popular thinking were made worse in the French case by fresh memories of experience in the early 1920's, when France had gone through a series of devaluations and bursts of inflation reacting on each other. The country broke out of this circle after 1926, and then failed to avoid an excessive dose of self-satisfaction about the great stability of the franc when the pound and the dollar were devalued early in the depression. By 1936, it would have been a good idea to correct the exchange rate even in the absence of the new social legislation. When it was actually changed, shortly after these reforms, it was easy to blame them for what looked like a sad blow to the country's prestige.

The combination of economic confusion, military threat, and animosity over new social legislation, proved too much for the Popular Front. The Blum Government fell after little more than a year, and successively more conservative cabinets went to work to modify the reforms. Labor

---

[3]Organization for European Economic Cooperation, *Industrial Statistics, 1900–1959,* (Paris: OEEC, 1960), p. 9.

tried to fight back with a general strike in 1938, but it was an utter failure. Both organized labor and business managed to convey the impression that their chief concern was to destroy the other, seriously weakening the society's cohesion on the eve of the war.

During the occupation of France, following its military defeat in 1940, the labor movement regained a good deal of the popular support it had lost in the years just prior to the war. Many labor leaders went into the resistance movement, others were imprisoned by the Germans as hostages, and efforts to force French workers to go to Germany against their will helped to identify labor as an opponent and victim of the enemy. On the other hand, too many French businessmen found it easy to cooperate with the Germans, saddling themselves with a reputation such that they had little or no political position left in the country at the time of the liberation. "Employers, practically taking to their cellars for safety, were absent from the great economic decisions of 1944–46."[4]

The immediate postwar government was a coalition that now sounds unbelievable. It was led by de Gaulle, with primary support by labor, with constructive participation by communist leaders insistent on improvement of efficiency and production, and with practically none of the country's traditional conservative elements. The beginning of economic planning, nationalization of many important companies, and a wide variety of social reform measures, were carried out swiftly. And once again, as in the case of the Popular Front, the reform government quickly fell apart. De Gaulle resigned in irritation at signs of renewed party politics in 1946. The Communist Party and the main labor confederation went back to war against the economic recovery drive in 1947. The old political parties and some new ones returned to struggle more over places in the government than over national policy, and the Fourth Republic wound its erratic way toward burial in 1958.

The political history of the 1950's is not inspiring. With momentary exceptions, it did not show much sign of progress. The economic history of the period is radically different. The economy literally woke up. The previous note of resigned protectionism, in what had seemed to be an incurably stagnant system, changed to insistence on growth. Emphasis on modernization and progress became almost as platitudinous as in the United States. The economy remained plagued by inflation, but in terms of output growth and structural transformation its performance turned out to be better than anything France has known for a very long time, if ever.

In the last few years, the economy has run into new difficulties. Problems of inflation and unemployment have become more troublesome, and

---

[4]Val R. Lorwin, *The French Labor Movement* (Cambridge, Mass.: Harvard University Press, 1954), p. 190.

the external balance has deteriorated. Judging from the explosion of mass irritation by students and workers in May, 1968, a significant proportion of the population distrusts the way the economy and the society are being run. They have plenty of grounds for complaint. But it would be wrong to think that the economy has fallen apart, or that future growth prospects are dark. The extraordinary performance of the economy through a full twenty years after the war strongly suggests that the mixture of policies adopted after Liberation contained highly positive features, and that the country does have the fundamental capacity for sustained growth whenever appropriate policies are adopted to stimulate it.

Agriculture 2

Agricultural policy before the war was consistently defensive, protective, and adverse for progress in the farm sector as in the whole economy. Postwar policy has been inconsistent, but better. It has included increasing effort to reorganize production, to develop exports, and to help farmers move into alternative occupations. These longer-range policies have been distinctly less popular with farmers than old-fashioned price supports, so supports have been generalized and raised. Improving efficiency combined with higher supports has led to production much in excess of markets at protected prices, complicating efforts to reach any rational set of mechanisms for agriculture within the Common Market. The magic balance between structural adjustment and short-run protection of farmers has not yet been found.

The Tradition of Protection

Natural conditions and human choice combined in the nineteenth century to keep France from following England's transition toward a specialized industrial economy relying on imports for most of its food. Resource advantages would have supported continuing importance for agriculture even with free trade. But, except for an interval from 1860 to the early 1880's, no one took any chances. As North American produc-

9

tion and cheaper transport brought down grain prices, French tariffs came back up to close the market.

With protection, small-scale farming was able to hang on. The number of farms kept growing until it reached a peak of about six million around 1890. Most farmers had to work with "tiny scattered parcels of land and to spend as much time traveling from one to another as in fruitful labor."[1]

The pressure of falling world prices for agricultural products might, if allowed to operate, have reduced the number of people in farming and led to improved methods. The French saw chiefly the other side of the coin: lower incomes for people in agriculture, and a forced change in the economic structure of the country. As in so many other contexts, they chose against change, shielding farmers from import competition and leaving poverty in the villages instead of driving it to the cities; relatively out of sight, and at least comforted by the familiar.

The Méline Tariff of 1892 has remained the symbol of the fundamental option for protection. Not because it represented the ultimate step in the process, or was significantly more restrictive than contemporary protectionism in the United States and elsewhere, but because it was a decisive turning point away from the open economy that then had strong advocates in France. It consecrated a coalition of agricultural and industrial interests opposed to free trade and helped to solidify the rigidities hampering modernization of the economy.[2]

Until the end of the 1920's, there was scarcely any content to agricultural policy other than the tariff system. The additions made then were at first concerned only with re-enforcing tariffs. A "milling ratio" for flour millers, requiring them to use French wheat for 97 percent of their supplies, was introduced in 1929. The ratio was raised to 100 percent in 1933. Quantitative import controls were adopted for a few products in 1931, and extended quickly to a wide range of both agricultural and industrial goods.[3]

When domestic demand continued to fall during the depression, merely shutting off outside producers proved to be an inadequate solution. The next steps, much like those in the United States, involved controls on production and sales by domestic producers themselves. From 1931, the government tried to organize markets for wine and for wheat. Licenses were required to sell wine, and the licenses were held down to levels intended to raise prices. Larger producers were forbidden to increase their vineyards, and were required to sell part of their output to a govern-

---

[1]Gordon Wright, *France in Modern Times* (Chicago: Rand McNally & Co., 1960), pp. 221-25, 359-62, quotation from p. 223.

[2]Daniel Salem, "Sur quelques conséquences du retour de la France au protectionnisme à la fin du xix⁰ siècle," *Revue d'histoire économique et social,* 1967, no. 3, pp. 326-80.

[3]Michael Tracy, *Agriculture in Western Europe* (New York: Frederick A. Praeger, Inc., 1964), pp. 124, 172-81.

ment office for distillation into alcohol and disposal. By 1937, the average price of wine was back up above the average for 1925-28. For wheat, the government set minimum legal prices, purchased part of the supply and made it unusable for consumption, and then added the less repulsive solution of export dumping.[4]

When the Popular Front Government entered in 1936, it advocated a more systematic approach to farm problems through a series of control offices to be run by joint producer-government committees. The only one actually adopted was the Wheat Office. Opposition to the proposed office was intense, but the argument was not concerned with control as opposed to free markets. It was simply the question of whether the producers or the government representatives would be the ones to run the office. "The crucial issue . . . was the locus of price-fixing power."[5] The farm organizations suspected that the Socialists intended to keep food prices down for the benefit of urban workers. They were finally bludgeoned into agreement by the threat of leaving prices up to the market. Their suspicions proved relevant. The government representatives did not accept the goal of higher prices automatically, and blocked some decisions that would have led in that direction.

The measures of control added in the 1930's were chiefly defensive reactions to the depression. The generalized deficiency of monetary demand made it seem intolerable to rely on market adjustments. Urban workers could not buy the food they wanted, and farmers whose output seemed unnecessary could not turn to any other production because there were no jobs. Shaping agricultural policy toward restriction of the food supply to keep up prices presented an unlovely but understandable picture.

Promotion of Structural Change

In the immediate postwar years, concern for surpluses and falling food prices was temporarily forgotten. Supplies were totally inadequate and prices went up rapidly. But controls on trade and domestic marketing were never abandoned. Instead they began, slowly and erratically, to be used as conscious instruments of economic policy directed toward changing resource use. Sometimes the only objective seemed to be that of price support and restriction, but gradually the element of structural reform began to grow in relative importance.

Some credit for the attempt to go in new directions should be given to the national economic plans. The First Plan, published in 1946, called for an increase of 25 percent in farm output, and for the development of

---

[4]*Ibid.*, pp. 174-78.

[5]Gordon Wright, *Rural Revolution in France* (Stanford: Stanford University Press, 1964), p. 62.

exports. The Planning Commission gave special aid to tractor producers to stimulate farm mechanization, and started a slow process of trying to get producer groups to reorient their thinking in terms of longer-run objectives instead of simple price support for whatever they happened to produce.[6] The central theme began to change from defensive preservation toward modernization and expansion.

There was room for improvement. As of 1950, real national income produced per worker in agriculture was only 35 percent of that for workers in other occupations.[7] And France still had an abnormally high proportion of its labor force in agriculture. That ratio had been the same as in the United States around 1880, at about half the active population. By 1950, the proportion had been brought down to 12 percent in the United States, but it was still 29 percent in France.[8] There were some modern farms, but they were a small minority. The median holding for which farming was the principal occupation was 26 acres.[9] While the larger units may well have been farmed as efficiently as anywhere else in the world, most of the manhours of work involved was spent on relatively small farms, overly diversified and badly chopped-up.

From the farmers' point of view, the main problem was that food prices began to fall relative to other goods as soon as immediate postwar shortages were met. The turning point came in 1949, when agricultural output got back to prewar levels. Pressure from farm interests to support food prices mounted quickly, running into direct conflict with two other policy objectives. One of them was the effort to stop inflation. The improvement in food supplies seemed at last to offer a chance to hold wages and prices down, but the farmers felt this made them the victims to be sacrificed. The other policy conflict was with the national economic plan. Its targets called for increasing agricultural production, not restricting it.

As all governments must do, some well and some less so, the French compromised. Minimum prices of wheat were raised, but at the same time imports of eggs, dairy products, and some vegetables were brought in deliberately to reduce their prices. The government returned to prewar techniques of buying up that part of the beet-sugar and wine supply considered to be excessive, turning both into alcohol, and then pouring that into the country's automobiles by mixing it with gasoline. Food prices went up, but more slowly than prices of industrial products. The Planning

---

[6] *Ibid.*, pp. 97, 144.

[7] Edward F. Denison and Jean-Pierre Poullier, *Why Growth Rates Differ* (Washington, D. C.: The Brookings Institution, 1967), 16-1, p. 204.

[8] *Ibid.*, Table 16-4, p. 206; Tracy, op. cit., p. 80; U.S. Department of Commerce, *Historical Statistics of the United States* (Washington, D. C.: Government Printing Office, 1960), p. 74.

[9] Institut National de la Statistique et des Études Économiques, *Annuaire statistique de la France, 1952* (Paris: Imprimerie Nationale, 1953), p. 84.

Commission held to its emphasis on increasing aggregate farm production, but in the second and third plans began to specify particular products which should be restrained: wine and oats in 1953, then wheat, sugar beets, and potatoes in 1958. The targets for expansion emphasized feed grains and livestock, considered particularly likely products for exports.[10]

Actual decisions on production and marketing were not subject to close control by the national plans. Administrative regulation operated in many markets, but methods and directions were usually determined by producers' organizations concerned chiefly with promoting higher prices. Alongside this "controlled" sector many markets remained totally unorganized, except for restrictions on imports. In the course of the 1950's, more and more markets—for dairy products, meat, and then several fruits and vegetables—were organized by producer groups with government support.

One of the most thoroughly controlled markets at all times has been that for beet sugar. The producers use some of the best land and most modern methods in French agriculture to produce too much of a product for which the value in world markets is almost always below their costs of production. Instead of forcing them to shift to other fields, the government accepted a continuation of the prewar system, using export subsidies and an agreement to buy excess supplies for distillation into alcohol. The Wheat Office of the 1930's, now expanded into a Cereals Office, likewise kept on with the depression system. The Office maintained a monopoly in foreign trade, required producers to sell through designated dealers, assigned quotas for wheat authorized to receive supported prices, and assigned taxes to producers in order to finance measures to get rid of the excess. Up to 1960, the taxes were set on a sliding scale intended to concentrate the penalty on the larger farms.[11]

Many smaller markets were thoroughly organized as well. The government tobacco monopoly set prices and the amounts that could be sold for all producers. The salt market involved thousands of producers but distribution was controlled by two firms, legally supported in a system that set prices to consumers about six times as high as those for sales to industrial buyers. Processors of Roquefort cheese continued to demonstrate the powers of a near-perfect oligopoly, built up over the course of nearly a century and supported by a law of 1925 limiting entry, to manage the final product market and set prices for some 8,000 suppliers.[12]

[10]Tracy, *op. cit.*, pp. 274-76.

[11]Organization for Economic Cooperation and Development, *Agricultural Policies in 1966* (Paris: OECD, 1967), p. 234.

[12]Jean Ousset, "La Concurrence imparfait dans les industries agricoles et alimentaires," in A. Piatier, *Les Formes modernes de la concurrence* (Paris: Gauthier-Villars, 1964), pp. 262-75.

Wine producers remained too numerous and dispersed to organize their own market; "consequently, it was done by the state."[13] New plantations were forbidden and high-yield grapes of low quality taken out of production by paying farmers to uproot the vines. Supplies declared to be excessive could be blocked from sale or purchased by the government for destruction. There was just one gap in the program for price stabilization: "excesses are disposed of, but deficits may occur and nothing is forseen for that case."[14]

Agricultural interests had always been well represented by legislators from farm areas and by professional pressure groups, but rarely with much more of a program than protectionism. These interests became much better organized in the course of the 1950's, particularly through the *Fédération Nationale des Syndicats d'Exploitants Agricoles* (FNSEA). The main force within the FNSEA was that of the larger farmers, more commercially oriented and chiefly interested in price supports. But an alternative line of policy gradually gathered more support from smaller farmers. They put more emphasis on credit for improved techniques, subsidies for mechanization, cooperatives to enable small farmers to share equipment, aid for movement to new areas and help in finding jobs for people interested in leaving agriculture, and extension of social-welfare legislation to the farm population.

The main expression of this newer approach came through the *Jeunesse Agricole Chrétienne*, established in the 1930's by the Catholic Church. The JAC took on a progressively more activist role in the 1950's, giving more weight to the interests of the smaller farmer in direct help or in aids to movement. They openly criticized both the standard solution of "prices first," and the fundamentalist notion of trying to keep as many people as possible in agriculture. In the course of the 1950's they began to capture leadership positions within the FNSEA and to provide support for more positive agricultural planning.[15]

The Third Plan, published in 1957, declared that a new approach to agricultural pricing was essential. "The products receiving the most encouragement in the way of prices and guaranteed markets are precisely those which, in view of the market situation, should be curtailed, while the products which should be encouraged are far from enjoying the same guarantees."[16] The plan introduced a system of "target prices," to move by stages from 1957 levels to specified goals for 1961. Changes in relative prices were designed to encourage potential exports, particularly meat, and to discourage production of wheat and wine.

---

[13]*Ibid.*, p. 307.
[14]*Ibid.*
[15]Wright, *Rural Revolution in France*, Ch. 8.
[16]Quoted from OECD, *Trends in Agricultural Policies Since 1955* (Paris: OECD, 1960), p. 138.

The methods to be used included all the market control techniques previously in force, plus systematic adjustment of imports and exports through state trading, import quotas, and export subsidies. The OECD published an illuminating summary of the export situation as of 1961, so understated as to make its implied criticism especially effective. "The need to organize the market for certain products in order to assure the stability of agricultural incomes has led to the introduction of a number of export aid schemes. Such exports are not, however, an essential purpose but are only an inevitable consequence of the organization of the national market and the regulation of prices. It is, therefore, a matter of using such procedures only for a few special products and for limited periods when the market is exceptionally unbalanced . . . The products for which export aids are currently provided are bacon and lard, dairy produce, cereals, sugar, some fruit and vegetables and certain fruit juices."[17]

The Common Market

Beginning in 1962, with the signing of the European Economic Community agreement on agricultural policy, questions of pricing and trade control moved into a wider context. The agreement established a goal of reaching a unified market by 1970. The way chosen to get there, and the intended relation of the European to the world market, seemed designed to be especially helpful to French agriculture.

Devaluation of the franc at the end of 1958, to permit entry into the Common Market, had brought French prices for wheat, barley, and beef below those in other member countries.[18] In general, German agricultural prices have been the highest of the group, and Germany has been the largest importer of food. In the absence of the Common Market, the importing countries might often buy French agricultural products, but would probably continue to get a high proportion of their imports from lower-priced outside sources. If the Market were completely closed to outsiders, the logic of resource allocation, and the actual set of relative prices, would greatly increase the role of French agriculture within the area.

The agreement does not predetermine the degree of self-sufficiency to be sought for the Common Market, though it is definitely intended that agricultural production inside the area be kept higher than it would be with an open system. Prices would be set above world market levels; if the latter fell, then import levies would move up automatically to insulate the Market. In the interim period to 1970, member countries would con-

---

[17]*Ibid.*, p. 153.
[18]Tracy, *op. cit.*, p. 327.

tinue to apply duties to imports from each other, but with a differential factor giving members preference over outside suppliers. The end result would be a situation of unified internal prices, with no levies or quantitative controls inside the group, and with the level of prices set by policy decision rather than world market conditions.

The level of prices to be chosen is a fundamental issue. If they are kept as much above world market levels as they have been in Germany, agricultural production in the whole area, especially in France, Italy, and the Netherlands will be encouraged despite high costs and regional imports will fall. The process would hold people in agriculture, diverting resources away from industrialization toward greater production of commodities which are of low value in world markets because they are already in abundant supply. It would have the further effect of restricting the main market for food exports now open both to North America and to the underdeveloped countries of the world.

French policy seems to be aimed at price levels above the outside world, but not as high as those in Germany. The target prices agreed to by the Council of Ministers of the EEC in July, 1966 ranged from 7 to 30 percent above the lowest levels then in effect in the countries with the largest production in the area, but remained below the highest in the deficit areas. In July, 1967 trade barriers were removed and common prices established for the principal grains (except for temporary permission to Italy to keep some levies on feed grains). For barley and soft wheat, German prices were brought down somewhat more than French prices were increased; for corn, the compromise was about even.[19]

The French and the EEC envisage some continuing imports of agricultural products for the area, to be approximately matched by food exports. Since the higher price level in the Market would require subsidies for exports, the French proposed to use the funds provided by import levies to pay for the export subsidies. This would mean that import taxes collected chiefly by Germany would subsidize exports coming mostly from France. The idea provoked dispute. The method now in effect is to use a central EEC fund for all forms of market support, including such subsidies, and to finance it jointly by import levies and direct budgetary contributions. For the latter, France contributes 32 percent of the total, and Germany, 31.2. The amounts of money involved are substantial; market support costs in 1967–68 are estimated at about $1.2 billion.[20] These costs, and the misdirection of effort they indicate, will clearly depend in the future on the degree to which the Market approaches self-sufficiency.

---

[19]U.S. Department of Agriculture, *Foreign Agriculture*, August 15, 1966, pp. 7-10 and December 4, 1967, pp. 7-8.

[20]*Ibid.*, October 31, 1966, p. 5.

Within France, a new *Loi d'Orientation Agricole* of 1960, and complementary legislation since, have moved several ambiguous steps toward more systematic overall policies. The theme of the legislation is that incomes in farming should be brought up to parity with those outside agriculture, but that this goal should be sought through long-run structural adjustments rather than merely by restrictions and price supports. Not that the latter have been disdained: the new rules extend producer group controls to more products and provide added legal backing for their efforts to "discipline" marketing procedures in order to maintain prices. But they also include more thorough definition of helpful and unhelpful forms of organizing markets, they centralize funds for market assistance to coordinate their use with the system of target prices, and they introduce greater support for research and structural reforms.[21]

In 1960, the government created a new agency, SAFER, to enter the market for farm land, buy up small plots and combine them into more efficient units, and invest in land improvements before selling farms back to private operation. The funds available for these operations have so far been too limited for any great impact, but as of 1965 about 300,000 acres had been "restructured" for more efficient operation in family-sized farms.[22]

The main forms of social welfare legislation, including medical insurance on terms equivalent to those for urban workers, and greatly improved retirement benefits, have finally been extended to farmers. The last step is of particular importance for all structural reform: many of the smaller farms that continue to hold on with outdated techniques are run by older people who have had no adequate alternative income or possibility of moving to new occupations. Giving them adequate retirement pensions should encourage a more rapid process of selling out smaller farms and converting them into larger units capable of giving better incomes to those who work them.

Expenditures in support of agriculture increased greatly between 1960 and 1965, from 4.2 to 9.2 billion francs. The fastest categories of growth have been for research and education, and for social security benefits to farmers. Total spending on research, plus advisory services and aid for improvement of farm structures and equipment, has been approximately double the amount of spending for market support.[23]

Lest one think that all has turned to rationality, it should be noted that the steps forward have been accompanied by odd turns and quirks. In deference to rules of the European Economic Community that forbid

---

[21]The complex and frequently revised rules applying to particular crops are summarized in OECD, *Agricultural Policies in 1966*, pp. 225-57.

[22]U.S. Department of Agriculture, *Foreign Agriculture*, September 5, 1966, pp. 3-4, and May 22, 1967, pp. 3-5.

[23]OECD, *Agricultural Policies in 1966*, p. 257.

arbitrarily uniform prices regardless of regional cost and transport differences, pricing methods that better reflect real costs have been introduced for cereals and poultry. But at the same time the state railroad
cut freight rates 30 percent on fruits and vegetables hauled from Brittany
in order to widen the market area for a region where farm incomes are
below the national average and farmers' abilities to organize belligerent
demonstrations are above average. While small poultry-raising operations
are being helped to reorganize into more efficient units, restrictive
licensing has been used to prevent industrial-type large-scale operations
threatening to undercut the costs of family farmers. The modernized
approach to price setting has its surprises too. For sugar, exceptionally
abundant production in 1960–61 forced an increase in storage operations
and export subsidies, so prices to consumers were raised to cover the
costs inflicted by abundant supply.[24]

It is possible to identify remaining areas of confusion, but there is a
fundamental change going on. People have finally begun to move rapidly
out of agriculture into activities in which their effort is more valuable.
It took about seventy years to bring the proportion of the labor force
working in agriculture down from half of the total to 29 percent, but
between 1950 and 1967 it fell from 29 to 16 percent.[25]

The shift of resources out of agriculture between 1950 and 1962 added
about 8 percent to national income.[26] Within agriculture, it certainly
facilitated reorganization of land holdings and improvement of techniques.
Between 1949 and 1959 output per man increased 61 percent; not as
rapidly as in Germany and Italy, but faster than in most other European
farm sectors, and more rapidly than in other sectors of the French
economy.[27]

The movement out of agriculture toward other occupations with higher
incomes acts both to increase the demand for food and to reduce the
number of farm families among which the value of sales is divided. The
Planning Commission estimates that real income per farm (value of
product divided by number of farms, corrected for the cost of living),
increased at a rate of 4 percent per year from 1954 to 1962.[28] When
the rate of gain slowed down to 2.5 percent for 1960–65, political pressures by farmers increased, and the government shifted back noticeably
from further efforts at technical reform to heavier support spending.

[24]*Ibid.*, pp. 238-40.
[25]Institut National de la Statistique et des Études Économiques, *Annuaire statistique
de la France, 1967* (Paris: Imprimerie Nationale, 1968), pp. 74-75.
[26]Denison, *op. cit.*, p. 211.
[27]Tracy, *op. cit.*, p. 277.
[28]*Cinquième Plan de dévelopment économique et social* (Paris: Imprimerie des Journaux
Officiels, 1965), Vol. 1, p. 191.

The Fifth Plan projected an annual rate of increase of real income per farm at 4.8 percent per year, better than any prolonged experience in the past, and better than the expected rate of growth of non-agricultural incomes for the planning period. Higher price supports helped to obtain this result for 1966 and 1967. But the expenditures involved were becoming overwhelming by 1968, because the high level of supports was beginning to generate production in excess of markets at those prices for practically everything. Since the same process has been going on throughout the Common Market, earlier forecasts of substantial French exports within the area have been generally revised downward. French wage costs in agriculture, while still below the costs that would allow agricultural workers to earn as much as those in industry, are now so much above those in Italy that it is hard to see how French production of those agricultural goods which require a great deal of labor, particularly fruit and vegetables, can possibly hold up in open competition.

The Common Market has been favorable for wheat and livestock producers, who are in general among the higher income groups within French agriculture. It has been least favorable for fruit, vegetable, and dairy farmers, who are often among the poorest. That is, it has at once exerted pressures consistent with desirable changes in the structure of production, and worsened inequalities of income within the sector. The way out would seem to lie through greater personal support of the poor farmers, and assistance for continued movement toward other occupations, combined with lower price supports. The recent trend toward persistently higher supports could, if continued, begin to weigh so heavily as to become a serious brake on the growth of the economy.

Postwar agricultural policies have been better than prewar, though perhaps not a great deal. The real difference since the war is that the non-agricultural sector has expanded so much more rapidly, raising demand for food and opening better opportunities for people to move into new occupations. The great failure in the preceding half-century was that the rest of the economy moved too slowly and left too many people stuck on farms. That failure was partly due to a single-minded insistence on protection, which has at least changed now toward greater attention to exports and increased concern with reduction of costs through improvement of methods of production. Agricultural policy seems to be moving past the stage of preventing change, toward more efficient high-income farming for fewer people, rather than continuing poverty for many.

Industry

3

Industry and government in France are interwoven to a far higher degree than they are in the United States. Investment plans of major companies are often discussed with government agencies able to help provide financing; the government tries to promote mergers and other changes in organization of private firms; and it owns quite a few companies outright. Direct regulation and selective intervention are common. It is not that the government is chiefly concerned with curbing the activities of private firms in order to ensure competition or to protect the public; it is more of an effort to push business toward faster modernization. There is no general consensus that business knows best and should be left alone. Instead, there is a widely shared belief that French industry is not naturally as progressive as it could be.

The mediocre performance of French industry prior to the war has often been blamed on excessive interference and protection by the government, and about equally as often on cultural or social factors acting to make businessmen themselves relatively unenterprising. The first interpretation implies that all would be well if the government let business alone, while the second suggests that the situation would be even worse if the government left decisions up to an excessively cautious private sector. Postwar experience brings out a possibility somewhat different than either of these interpretations. When intervention by the government changed toward promotion rather than protection, providing a more expansionary environment, many sectors of private industry began to adopt more dynamic policies in response. The real problem before the war may have been chiefly that the government shared the same protectionist attitudes as private industry. Its style of intervention was no help at all, but it did not so much block otherwise dynamic forces as reenforce the orientation of private industry by providing badly designed incentives. That interpretation does not suggest either that the best results could be achieved by stopping intervention, or that the government needs to run things in detail, but that better incentives could generate more positive responses overcoming cultural factors relatively unfavorable for expansion.

Industrial Structure and Behavior

By such simple tests as output per man, or capacity to export industrial goods, France is among the leading countries in the world. But it is much further down the list than it was a century ago; it declined from original leadership in industrialization and scientific progress to a position of distinctly reduced importance.

Manufacturing industries produced 37 percent of gross national product in 1962, compared to an average of 30 percent for all OECD countries, or to 28 percent for the United States.[1] The high ratio in France is a result of both positive and negative factors. On the positive side, it represents a successful transition from the economy's earlier dependence on agriculture, a move up the world scale of modernization. On the other side, it reflects the relative slowness with which this transition, well under way in the first half of the nineteenth century, was carried out between then and the second world war. If the move away from agriculture had been accomplished more rapidly, France could have passed through the stage of such concentration on manufacturing by now, and shifted toward greater emphasis on professional employment and service occupations. This latter trend is now under way: the proportion of the labor force employed in industry increased between 1954 and 1962, but the proportion employed in services increased slightly faster.[2]

As industrial production increased during the century up to the Second World War, its composition changed much more slowly than in competing countries. It was not that the country lacked eminent scientists or imaginative inventors. "At the beginning of the century, France was undoubtedly the vanguard of scientific progress. Paris was a pole of attrac-

---

[1] Organization for Economic Cooperation and Development, *Industrial Statistics, 1900–1962* (Paris: OECD, 1964), p. 3.

[2] Samuel Baum, "The World's Labour Force and Its Industrial Distribution, 1950 and 1960," *International Labour Review*, Jan.–Feb. 1967, p. 111.

tion for researchers the world over . . . up to 1935, out of a total of 111 Nobel prizes for physics, chemistry, and physiology, 16 were awarded to French scientists." The trouble was that the industrial sector, although receptive to new ideas, usually tried them so cautiously, on such small scales, that other countries often took away the lead in reducing costs or improving on the original notion. The French were often unable to compete in fields that they had themselves originated.

One early example was that of the field of organic chemistry, in which French scientists got an early start and then nearly gave up completely. A new company was established in 1863 to produce the first synthetic dye developed in France. It obtained a monopoly patent, and then discovered that others were able to improve the basic idea to get lower costs and develop further synthetic dyes. Instead of trying to get ahead of them through continued research, the company with the patent concentrated its effort on blocking production by others. The result was to drive most of the technicians and producers concerned to Switzerland, where they largely created the Swiss chemical industry. The company then went broke because it could not compete with foreign dyes smuggled back into France.[4]

French and American inventors discovered the electrolytic reduction process basic to the modern aluminum industry almost simultaneously in 1886, but the company then producing aluminum in France decided not to bother adopting the new process because the old one, though much more expensive, seemed good enough for a product with such a limited market. Much of the success of du Pont in the United States with cellophane and rayon, and its subsequent lead in synthetic fabrics, was based on French inventions which were not rapidly exploited in their home country. A French inventor worked out the fundamentals of fluorescent lighting in the early 1920's, but the producer failed to take it past limited use in advertising signs; the standard fluorescent lamp had to await simple modifications by General Electric in the United States a decade later, and then a competitive threat from Sylvania to force General Electric into large-scale marketing.[5] The difference in France was double: the firm with the leading position did not try to adapt the product for mass use, and business behavioral patterns were such that no rival firm forced the pace.

As of 1913, the French accounted for about 13 percent of manufacturing production in Europe; their shares of steel production, of chemicals, and of cotton consumption by the textile industry, were all between 11 and 14 percent. But for machinery production, where frequent techno-

---

[3]OECD, *Reviews of National Science Policy: France* (Paris: OECD, 1966), p. 19.

[4]Paul M. Hohenberg, *Chemicals in Western Europe: 1850–1914* (Chicago: Rand McNally & Co., 1967), pp. 35-36 and 41.

[5]Arthur A. Bright, Jr., *The Electric Lamp Industry* (New York: The Macmillan Co., 1949), pp. 381-98.

logical change would be essential to take advantage of continuously emerging possibilities, it was only 5 percent. Exports of manufactured products by the eight leading industrial exporters in that year included 16 percent in "expanding" fields such as machinery and transport equipment, and 58 percent in older, "contracting" groups. The distribution of French exports of manufactured products included only 10 percent in the expanding fields, and 74 percent in those classified as contracting.[6]

The tendency to stick to older lines of production was associated with an apparent reluctance to go beyond the relatively small-scale family firm. No one has ever accused French businessmen of being uninterested in making more money, but they seem to have given unusually high weight to motives that ran against profit-maximization when it involved any possibility of losing control of the firm. The social prestige of ownership, and perhaps also the security it afforded for members of families ill-equipped to achieve high earnings on their own, discouraged recourse to outside financing more in France than in other industrial countries. Cultural patterns "motivated businessmen toward caution, thrift, security, tradition, avoidance of risk—toward running the business as an annuity, maximizing security rather than profits, growth, output, or any combination thereof." French business was "a system built around small units, small volume, and small horizons."[7]

International comparisons of the size of plants are subject to many problems of interpretation, but studies of French industries have been consistent in finding a bias toward operation on smaller scales than in counterpart industries in other countries. One of the best of such investigations, using an ingenious corrective device to take account of differences in national statistics for the smallest companies, showed that only 28 percent of workers in manufacturing were employed in plants with over a thousand employees in 1954, compared to 38 percent in Germany and 31 percent in both Italy and Belgium. The average number of employees per plant in the French textile industry was about 295, compared to 395 in Germany and 405 in Italy.[8]

While there is little doubt that French business was relatively reluctant to abandon family-owned firms and to take risks for expansion, the range of behavior has always been wide, including examples to fit any thesis one might wish to advocate. It is quite possible that the abundant liter-

---

[6]Ingvar Svennilson, *Growth and Stagnation in the European Economy* (Geneva: United Nations, 1954), pp. 16 and 295.

[7]John E. Sawyer, "The Entrepreneur and the Social Order, France and the United States," in William Miller, ed., *Men in Business* (Cambridge, Mass.: Harvard University Press, 1952), pp. 14 and 17. Cf. Charles P. Kindleberger, *Economic Growth in France and Britain, 1851–1960* (Cambridge, Mass.: Harvard University Press, 1964), pp. 115-23.

[8]P. L. Mandy and Guy de Ghellinck, "La Structure de la dimension des entreprises dans les pays du Marché Commun," *Revue économique*, May 1960, pp. 406 and 410-411. For a review of many such comparisons, cf. Kindleberger, *loc cit.*

ature on peculiarly French attitudes takes a grain of truth too far. The more important consideration may be that nothing was ever done to exert any competitive pressure on the more backward firms, either from outside the country or inside it. Business owners could permit themselves the luxury of inefficiency because consumers were prevented from buying newer or cheaper products from other countries.

American industry grew up under protection too, but generated its own substitute for import competition. The values of the society, expressed both in law and in the attitudes of businessmen, favored encouragement of these firms which tried to grow and to establish new methods. The American approach can rightly be criticized for failure to help weaker firms transform and keep up with change; the French, for the opposite tendency, to preserve the weak from any necessity of change at all. According to Léon Blum, "the law of French capitalism seems to be to prevent the death of antiquated enterprise."[9]

Competition was always possible in France, it simply did not happen to be a preferred form of conduct. Cartel agreements were accepted and widely used.[10] Ancient laws against monopoly were periodically restated, but there was no enforcement agency comparable to the Federal Trade Commission or the Anti-Trust Division to give them meaning. The general preference for preservation of all producers rather than for promoting competition among them was frequently expressed in laws handicapping larger companies. Taxation was persistently biased against larger companies in the prewar period, and administrative regulations often were used in the same way. The system sacrificed efficiency for protection.

At Liberation in 1944, the sense of impatience at past economic performance and of eagerness to try something new was so widely shared that no political force stood out against radical change. The traditional parties were disorganized, with their more conservative elements temporarily paralyzed. It became, for a brief period, easy to carry through changes meant to be revolutionary. In the event, the reform programs of the period 1944–46 did not turn out to constitute any fundamental overturn of the economic system, but they embodied many changes that would sound dramatic if proposed in the United States today. A series of nationalizations brought in government ownership of the leading banks, the coal mines and the electric power and gas industries, Air France, and the Renault automobile company. Price controls were continued into the postwar period and collective bargaining over wages was suspended (until 1950). Economic planning started and the banking system began to operate selective credit controls intended to direct investment along lines favored by the plans.

---

[9]Quoted in Herbert Luethy, *France Against Herself* (New York: Meridian Books, 1957), p. 314.

[10]Henry W. Ehrmann, *Organized Business in France* (Princeton, N.J.: Princeton University Press, 1957), Ch. 8.

The new measures were intended to modernize the economy rapidly. To some, that meant a repudiation of capitalism. Central planning and government ownership in "strategic sectors" could be considered as steps toward complete control of private industry. To others, it meant an attack on the traditional weaknesses of capitalism as practiced in France, in order to promote more vigorous growth by a combination of public and private initiative. In practice, the economy has followed the second of these two paths, with renewed growth of the private sector rather than its disappearance or subjugation.

Government Ownership

Nationalization and public ownership sound perhaps the most radical of all the new measures. They turned out to be helpful in some cases and not in others, but in general to have much more modest consequences than anticipated. The managers of the new corporations owned by the government quickly began to act much like those of private corporations, trying to get rid of unprofitable activities, to insist on the need of adequate prices and profits for investment, and above all to resist governmental intrusion in their operations. They demonstrated fairly well that orientation toward profit remains an essential aspect of rational management even when there are no capitalists in the picture.

The discovery that publicly owned corporations acted much like privately owned corporations surprised people to such an extent that it tended to obscure another important consideration: that they acted more like modern corporations than like traditional French business. They were not any less interested in profits. The difference was rather that most of them proved more dynamic and imaginative in trying to raise earnings than private business had previously been. This was not true of all of them. The newly nationalized commercial banks continued to act just as routinely as they had under private ownership, and the publicly owned telephone service has yet to show any marked sign of initiative. But the nationalized electric power and railroad systems proved highly progressive, and the automobile company taken over by the government turned out to be the most expansionary firm in one of the country's most dynamic and competitive industries.

Most of the nationalizations involved firms in fields usually considered to be public utilities, such as electricity, gas, and railroads. These public corporations were given monopoly positions, as were the nationalized coal mines. Others remained in competition with private firms: Renault, the government companies involved in production of aircraft frames and engines, oil companies, and a fertilizer producer since converted into a chemical company.

In the monopoly fields, the government corporations have frequently been unprofitable and have required substantial subsidies. For electricity, gas, and the railroads, the problem has not been one of inefficiency on the part of the companies, but rather that the Ministry of Finance has often blocked rate increases in the interest of stabilizing the price index. The companies could not be left to set their own prices, because they always have good reasons for new expenditures that would require more earnings, and they are not subject to any strict check from competition. The issue is the same as that with respect to regulated private utilities in the United States, except that the state monopolies have had a tougher time raising rates than our private companies usually do.

For the coal mines, deficits have been continuous and have been a meaningful indication of inefficiency, though not inefficiency in the sense of poor management. Nationalization permitted extensive reorganization of production, closing of old mines, and extremely rapid gains in productivity. The efficiency in question is rather that of the country's use of resources. With all the rationalization and mechanization that has been accomplished, it has been necessary at times to price coal below marginal costs in order to sell it.[11] Its internal price is more than half again as high as that of possible imports. The industry under public ownership has made more of an effort at internal efficiency than it did under private ownership before the war, but if it had been exposed either to open market forces or to planned rationality it would probably have shut down many more of its operations.

As compared to their earlier private counterparts in France, the newly created government monopolies have been more concerned with high investment and rationalization in the sense of improving technical criteria of performance. This has had good consequences for efficiency of service, and negative consequences in stimulating too much capital-intensive investment in the early postwar period of capital shortage. Some of them, particularly the *Électricité de France* and the *Société Nationale des Chemins de Fer*, have become renowned for the high level of technical analysis they have learned to apply to problems of devising rational price structures or choosing investment projects. The railroad system runs much better than ours, which is perhaps faint praise but worth noting. On the other hand, the telephone system, under government ownership from its inception, works very poorly. This may be related to an organizational defect not inherent in public ownership per se: the telephone service has not had the status of an independent corporation, but has instead been a sideline of the postal service.

In those cases in which government firms have been in competition

---

[11]Pierre Bauchet, *Proprieté publique et planification* (Paris: Éditions Cujas, 1962), pp. 197-98.

with private companies, both sides have survived the experience and there have been some highly interesting results. In the oil industry, the government firms have participated whole-heartedly in domestic cartel-type selling arrangements. Outside France, they have acted more independently relative to the world industry, but political factors play such a major role that economic implications are unclear, to say the least. Political factors also confuse the picture with respect to the aviation industry. There are two particularly impressive firms, one completely private (Dassault), and one owned by the government (Sud Aviation). Sud Aviation was so well run that Chrysler hired away its president to take over Simca, its subsidiary in the French automobile industry. That industry presents the most interesting case of all, because it is more nearly free of any special political entanglements, and it has been a leader in postwar industrial change.

Renault was nationalized almost by accident, as a punishment for alleged wartime collaboration by its owner. It had been the third largest producer before the war; as a government corporation, it soon became the first.[12] It was the first French automobile producer to break out of familiar markets and take up exporting on a significant scale. It has remained the leading exporter of the industry throughout the last decade. It specialized on production of lighter economy cars until the early 1960's, got caught behind temporarily when public tastes began to change with rising incomes, but then broadened its model range and renewed rapid expansion in the last few years. It pioneered application of automatic transfer methods in French industry in the early postwar years, developing its own machines for the purpose, and also pioneered significant changes in labor relations designed to promote more company-oriented, less political, methods of collective bargaining.

Renault always insisted on its independence from government intervention in its decisions, and was able to get away with it because it did not need subsidies. It paid the same taxes as other firms, and regularly paid a part of its profits to the government. If it had any unfair advantage over the private firms, it was in relative freedom from restrictions imposed by extra-economic objectives of its owners. Renault has been at least as free as the other companies, and in some respects more enterprising.

In terms of profits, Renault has not done as well as Peugeot. Company statements do not always make the profit position clear—Citroën in particular has been almost fanatically secretive—but Peugeot has been able to maintain a good rate of growth, encroaching on Citroën for second place in the industry, while generating internal funds greatly in

---

[12]John Sheahan, *Promotion and Control of Industry in Postwar France* (Cambridge, Mass.: Harvard University Press, 1963), Ch. 7.

excess of investment requirements.[13] Peugeot also followed Renault's lead in turning to exports more vigorously than the other two private companies did, and joined Renault in developing dealer facilities to support exports. It is still a closely owned family firm, but that has not prevented dynamic behavior.

Citroën, on the contrary, never made much of an attempt to stress expansion and exports. Its models have been technically the most imaginative in the industry, and its management among the least. By 1968, its financial problems became so difficult that its owner, Michelin, tried to arrange a merger with Fiat. The case underlined the degree to which the government considers itself entitled to oversee major business decisions: it simply refused to allow the sale of control to Fiat. On the other hand, the government has stopped short of forcing what it clearly would prefer: that all three of the French-owned companies merge together.

Public ownership in French industry has been less revolutionary than one might expect. It has done some good: precisely the kind of good that more dynamic private industry could have done itself, but which French private industry sometimes did not do. As most private industries have become a good deal more dynamic since the war, serious political support of further nationalization has greatly weakened. None of the postwar nationalizations has been undone, but no new ones have been carried out since 1946.

Planning at the Industry Level

The introduction of national economic planning in 1946 represented a broader vision and constituted a more enduring line of policy than nationalization of private firms. It has had many ramifications going well beyond the industrial sector, but at first it was concentrated on modernization of particular industries.

From the start, planning was intended to work through joint government-industry consultation. Industries were never given orders by the Planning Commission. They were asked to discuss investment programs, and offered low-interest loans, as well as administrative cooperation from the Commission, for adoption of approved projects. They remained free to reject such advice when they wished, or to go ahead with different programs of their own. Targets for production never had the status of requirements in the sense of Russian planning; they were usually no more than indicators of expected markets. The idea was to clarify the pattern of decisions by industries that would be consistent

---

[13]*Etudes et conjoncture,* "Les comptes des sociétés de quelques grands secteurs industriels, 1955–64," Sept. 1967, p. 115.

with a high rate of overall growth, and to rely on mutual interest plus subsidized loans to encourage the actions indicated by the plans.

In the first phase, immediately after the war, use of credit for investment by the commercial sector and by older consumer goods industries, as well as in housing construction, was selectively limited to facilitate greater investment by favored producer-goods industries. The Commission set production targets to guide investment by these industries, helped them to get capital, and generally left questions of internal organization up to them.

The one significant exception was that of the steel industry during the First Plan. When the Commission asked the companies to formulate investment proposals to meet production targets, the replies indicated that most companies intended to rebuild plants in much the same locations, to provide the same product mix, with the same scale of plants as before the war. The Commission rejected this approach, and prepared a detailed program calling for concentration of facilities in larger plants capable of using modern techniques to full advantage. The leading firms did in general follow the Commission's program. Two modern mills were installed where specified, several firms consolidated into larger units, and some higher-cost facilities were shut down. Progress toward greater specialization and concentration among the smaller producers was extremely slow at first. It speeded up after 1952, when adoption of the Schuman Plan began to allow imports of steel to bring competitive pressure on producers inside France.

The fields given particular attention in the first period of planning, including steel, did in some respects stand out in their performance. But by the middle 1950's the more striking success stories came in a group of industries that was not favored in the plans: production of durable consumers goods. As this process developed, the Planning Commission shifted away from detailed industry programs toward increasing concern with social goals and overall economic policy. These aspects of the more recent plans are discussed in Chapter 6.

Postwar Changes in Demand and in Producer Behavior

The most evident change in consumption patterns has been the mass adoption of the automobile. In 1949, only 8 percent of French families had an automobile; by 1966, the proportion was 48 percent. Similarly, wives began to enter the world of household electrical equipment. Between 1952 and 1959, production of refrigerators quadrupled and that of washing machines tripled. High employment generated rapidly rising consumer demand, at income levels appropriate for widespread adoption of durable goods. The structure of demand had an important connotation for efficiency and costs. These industries in general had been operating at scales far too low for reasonable efficiency, so were perfectly placed to reap the benefits of significant economies of scale when the wave of postwar consumer demand hit them; they were able to provide rapidly increasing output with greatly improving productivity.

The exceptional opportunities of the mass-production consumer goods industries in the 1950's were by no means automatically translated into demand-determined rates of growth. The automobile industry outperformed even the excellent growth possibilities provided by the domestic market, developing exports which rose to a fourth of total production in 1963 and 1964. Producers of refrigerators did much less well. Although output expanded rapidly in the 1950's, costs and prices remained relatively high. After the reduction of trade barriers in the Common Market, Italian producers entered successfully to capture most of the gain in sales made possible by further growth of demand.

Perhaps the outstanding characteristic of French industry in the 1950's became its markedly greater capacity to change. Production shifted significantly to new plant locations, old industries contracted and released labor to expanding sectors, and the backlog of excessive numbers of producers in nearly all fields began to be corrected. The process was given a shove in the right direction by the Planning Commission in the immediate postwar period, but then began to operate more on its own, under the joint stimulus of increased competition and persistently favorable aggregate demand.

At the end of 1963, employment in new industrial plants established between 1954 and 1962 was six times as great as the increase in employment in all the plants which had existed in 1954.[14] The new establishments were generally concentrated in the fields of fastest growth; they accounted for 50 percent of employment in electrical machinery and equipment. These data include new subsidiaries of existing firms, both French and foreign, but they still suggest a more flexible and widening entrepreneurial response than anything observable in France prior to the war.

At the same time, many old producers were being weeded out. The census of 1954 listed 642,721 industrial establishments. By 1962, with production 62 percent higher, there were 518,742.[15] The reductions were

---

[14]Alain d'Iribarne, "La Population des établissements nouveaux," *Revue économique,* Nov. 1967, pp. 975-1037. These data refer to new "establishments," which means plants built in new locations, whether by new firms or as branches or subsidiaries of existing companies. The data used exclude construction, leave out plants with fewer than ten workers, and also do not cover either the Paris region or Champagne-Picardy.

[15]Institut National de la Statistique et des Études Économiques, *Les Établissments industriels et commerciaux en France en 1954,* pp. 60-75, and *Annuaire statistique de la France, 1966* (Paris: INSEE, 1966), p. 209. These data exclude the construction industry.

particularly striking in the more highly decentralized fields, notably textiles and "general mechanical industries." The number of establishments in textile production fell 24 percent. This was not entirely a market process. The industry came under increasing competitive pressure with the advent of the Common Market, but it also operated its own system of taxation to raise funds to buy out and destroy capacity of companies willing to shut down. The market was the motor force, but it was not left to operate unaided.

The government took some steps to encourage competition in 1953. A commission was created to study agreements among firms, and retail price maintenance was made illegal.[16] The commission was given a legal framework very different from that of American antitrust law. Agreements were not assumed to be bad, but were to be studied on a case-by-case basis to identify those which improved efficiency and those which might be harmful. The commission apparently did not find many that were harmful, and its activities did not have a great impact on the economy. The elimination of retail price maintenance may have been a more important step. It came at a most opportune time, when chain stores and discount operations were beginning to undermine traditional retailing methods. The rapid growth of the newer types of stores in the last decade probably owes a good deal to the freedom given them to put pressure on suppliers and to offer standardized goods at prices below those common in smaller stores.

A crucial change favoring competition was the reduction of barriers against imports, starting with the Coal-Steel Community in 1952 and following with entry into the Common Market at the end of 1958. The official French position in the Market has been opposed to extension of membership, and has generally favored retention of high external tariffs, but it has also favored rapid reduction of barriers within the group. At the beginning of July, 1968, the last tariffs on industrial imports from member countries were removed.

Common Market competition would have been fatal to French industry at original price levels, but the government carried out an unusually successful devaluation just before entering, which made French industry strongly competitive at the start. Exports responded well. The proportion of French industrial production sold to countries outside the franc zone rose from 9 percent in 1954 to 12 percent by 1959, and then to 18 percent by 1966.[17] Similarly, domestic consumers were able to buy a higher proportion of their manufactured goods from other countries. In 1966,

---

[16]Jacques Houssiaux, *Le Pouvoir de monopole* (Paris: Éditions Sirey, 1958), pp. 201-207.

[17]Sheahan, *op. cit.*, p. 159; *Rapport sur les comptes de la nation de l'année 1966* (Paris: Imprimerie Nationale, 1967), p. 456.

total exports of manufactured goods (to countries in the franc zone as
well as to competitive markets), equalled 21 percent of production, while
total imports equaled 19 percent of production. The relatively closed-in
economy of the prewar period has been replaced by one much more open
to the outside world, with a greater competitive stimulus for producers
and a much wider range of choice for consumers.

Concentration

Administrative techniques of intervention, which were almost always
used before the war to favor smaller companies, have in general been
turned around to help the larger firms, particularly those cooperating
with the plans. In some ways this change improved flexibility and favored
greater efficiency. But it has come to constitute an automatic bias in
favor of large size, without regard to the possibilities of negative effects.

The change to active encouragement of large size is a form of compensation for prewar errors in the opposite direction. There is little question that much of the country's production is carried out in plants too
small to realize technologically possible economies, nor that research and
development are handicapped by insufficient financing and scale. If the
government were to improve financing possibilities for research and
development, maintain favorable demand conditions and an appropriate
exchange rate, and remove artificial measures protecting small companies,
the country would get both larger firms and better performance. That
process has been a significant part of postwar economic improvement.
But on top of it, especially in the 1960's, the government has added both
selective incentives and direct pressures to make the firms that are already
among the largest in the country merge with each other.

The Fifth Plan recommended, and the government adopted, a series
of special tax incentives and administrative measures to promote mergers
during the planning period, on little more than the general premise that
bigger companies are better. Mergers among major companies reported
in the financial press increased gradually up to 1966; in that year there
were more than in the entire preceding decade. In 1967 the number fell
off, but the average size of the firms involved more than doubled. They
have featured the largest firms in the country, merging among each other.
In 1966, a merger made Thomson-Houston-Hotchkiss-Brandt the twelfth
largest firm in the economy and the second largest in electrical equipment;
in 1967 it tacked on CSF, the leading producer of electronics and the
number twenty-six French firm by sales volume. Pechiney, the dominant
aluminum producer, and involved in many other fields, joined its chemical
operations with St. Gobain, the leading European glass producer. It

then merged in 1967 with Tréfimetaux, thus linking closely three companies that were each separately among the largest 25 firms in France.[18]

Even the largest of the new mergers leave the resulting companies on a much smaller scale than the giants of American industry. That fact continues to dominate policy on the subject, without much attention to the consideration that the number of centers of independent research and initiative, on scales sufficient to make a difference, may be reduced in the merger process. If one starts from the premise that too many producers operate with very small plants, it is not evident that the cure is to take the largest firms in the country and merge them into each other. The gain might be significant if the management of some of the merger partners were particularly weak, and could be eased out of control in the process. That is clearly the intention in some cases. In many others the result may be little more than to put two sets of managers, not particularly dynamic in the first place, jointly in charge of a bigger problem than they were previously able to handle well on a smaller scale. The policy has confused the goal—large firms which grow because of superior performance—with size itself.

American Investment and the Technological Race

Investment in France by American firms was relatively unimportant until the middle 1950's, but it rose very rapidly thereafter as the economy's growth capacity became clearer. It took a form not commonly followed by international capital placements among European countries. Where Belgian, Swiss and other foreign investors usually bought securities, American firms either bought French companies outright or established wholly-owned subsidiaries for production. Further, American firms concentrated particularly on those industries associated with technological advances that French business had been slow to develop. IBM-France became the symbol of American dominance in modern technology. The general uneasiness of French industry and the government was greatly aggravated by the fact that the one national firm which had made significant progress in the computer industry, Machines Bull, ran into financial difficulties and had to sell a 50 percent interest to the American General Electric Company. It looked as if the leading sectors of modern industry in France were likely to be dominated by the United States.

Fears that France would be totally outclassed in fields vital to future

---

[18]Size rankings in terms of sales for 1965 and 1966 are given in Chase Manhattan Bank, *World Business*, Sept. 1967, pp. 8-9. Merger data from the *Economist*, Nov. 4, 1967, p. 558, also Jacques Houssiaux, "Les Fusions et concentrations d'entreprises en France en 1967," and A.P. Weber, "Analyse générale des fusions et concentrations d'entreprises en 1967," *Direction*, March 1968, pp. 254-61.

industrial growth led to two kinds of reactions. One was wholly negative. From 1963 to 1966 official policy discouraged applications by American firms wishing to invest in France. This did not work out well. The companies concerned went to Belgium or Germany instead, creating new jobs and exports, and helping spread understanding of new technologies there rather than in France. Since 1966, the policy has been reconsidered and made more favorable for possible investment.

The other reaction to this inflow of American firms was more forward-looking. The government began to promote scientific and industrial research more actively, and French firms themselves began to pay greater attention to the need for research programs. The change in thinking was caught and most effectively publicized by a surprising best-seller in 1967, *Le Défi américain*.[19] The theme of the book was that American firms were able to lead European companies in taking advantage of the Common Market because of more flexible managerial techniques focused on research and innovation. The difficulty on the French side was ascribed to over-centralization in decisions, and more fundamentally to an educational and social system that discouraged initiative and failed to develop the nation's potential for change. France had managed to go some way from the old family firm to the *forms* of modern corporate industry, but had retained the substance of excessively centralized decision making characteristic of prewar industry.[20]

The fact that industrial research and the development of industries based on scientific progress have been lagging is perhaps best seen as a consequence of such managerial weaknesses, but it was compounded by a singular failure of the planning process and government policy in general. Loans for modernization and the many other devices for industrial promotion were focused on older industries—those which formed the core of an up-to-date economy prior to the 1950's—while research and scientific development were relatively neglected.

Combined public and private research expenditures were about 0.8 percent of GNP in 1959. A thorough reorganization of governmental research agencies in 1958, increasing concern by private industry, and stress on this area in the Fourth Plan, helped to double this ratio by 1965. It was then slightly above the ratio for Germany, distinctly below that in the United Kingdom, and about half that in the United States. In absolute terms, research expenditures in the United States were about fifteen times those in France, and the ratio of scientists and engineers

---

[19]Jean-Jacques Servan-Schreiber (Paris: Denoël, 1967), translated as *The American Challenge* (New York: Atheneum, 1968). For an excellent American discussion of the same issues, see Robert Gilpin, *France in the Age of the Scientific State* (Princeton, 1968).

[20]Servan-Schreiber, *op. cit.*, especially Ch. 20; Francois Bloch-Lainé, *Pour une reforme de l'entreprise* (Paris: Editions du Seuil, 1963).

available in the two countries was about 12 to 1.[21] American industrialists ask for tariff protection because of cheap foreign labor; French industrialists explain their wish to block competition from American firms in terms of their disadvantage in research and technical knowledge.

In overall terms, the government finances about two-thirds of all research, and industry one-third. These are the same proportions as in the United States. In both countries, the total is dominated by defense or atomic development activities. "Economically motivated" research is relatively low for both. In 1965, it was 41 percent of the total in France, compared to 51 percent in the United Kingdom and 62 percent in Germany.[22] For an economy presumably being guided by plans focused on modernization, the results in terms of research do not seem impressive.

Current attempts to stimulate research in the most advanced fields raise a difficult issue of resource allocation. They typically require extremely costly investment, and people who are not so much pure scientists as technicians capable of translating scientific ideas into workable industrial practices. France is not exceptionally rich in either resource. Furthermore, the structure of demand at present income levels is directed toward more standardized industrial goods with known technologies. The country is generally able to compete with foreign producers in such fields, but has no great lead suggesting that it can easily afford to devote its best people to currently non-commercial activities. That is, it might pay better in the near future to out-compete in automobiles and television, and to concentrate advanced research in some area where the country has a relatively good initial basis (such as aviation), rather than to try to get ahead in every area of scientific advance at once. The present preference may represent an overly generalized compensation for past omissions.

As far as the industrial structure is concerned, the chances of translating new ideas into rising efficiency and innovation have been greatly improved. Companies uninterested in keeping up with change no longer get special protection but instead run into toughening import competition and government advice to sell out or change lines of production. If they are small and keep unclear books to escape taxes, their former advantage over the better organized companies is now offset by special help the latter can get for investment. And all those interested in new products and expansion have had, with brief exceptions, the enormous aid of an economy growing around them to improve opportunities.

---

[21]OECD, *Review of National Science Policy: France* (Paris: OECD, 1966), p. 31: also, *The Overall Level and Structure of R & D Efforts in OECD Member Countries* (Paris: OECD, 1967), pp. 14, 20-21.

[22]OECD, *The Overall Level and Structure of R & D Efforts, op. cit.*, p. 58.

Labor

4

French workers sound and act fundamentally dissatisfied. If they were asked to vote on a proposition to confiscate all of private industry, preferably without compensation, there is an excellent chance that the proposition would win. Negative attitudes have not taken the form of strong union organization or activity, but rather of prolonged apathy. Most of the time, unions in the private sector seem weak and inept. But once in a great while, as in 1936 and 1968, some spark wakes everyone up, and workers seize plants across the country with great enthusiasm.

The generally negative positions of workers toward both business and the government are sometimes explained in terms of historical forces and ideology, as if they had little or no relation to current reality.[1] There is a good deal to that idea: the French have an unusual capacity to see the present through the past, to look at events through a mental frame that predetermines what will be seen. But that does not mean that attitudes are eternally immune to changes in external reality. Few people any longer try to sell the idea that workers are being progressively impoverished; cherished as that thesis is to elderly Marxists, real wages have been going up so rapidly for so long that its reiteration now is recognized to be ridiculous. The trouble is rather that reality still includes many

---

[1]Cf. Richard F. Hamilton, *Affluence and the French Worker in the Fourth Republic* (Princeton, 1967).

genuine grounds for frustration. The right of unions to negotiate bilaterally on wages and working conditions is barely on the borderline of possible acceptance as far as many French industrialists are concerned; many are still using tactics of resistance that sound quaintly amusing when described in histories of the nineteenth century, and downright pathological now. Workers do not feel that they are represented in the political process, and that is correct. Their children do not share equally in opportunities for higher education and entry into the key positions of the society. The tax system is biased toward protection of property incomes. A worker at age 35 has the same remaining life expectancy as a teacher at age 47. It is not so much that workers have an unshakable capacity to ignore favorable facts as it is a matter of exceedingly slow improvement in the facts themselves.

The National Confederations

The unions that one hears about most of the time in France are the national confederations, rather than industry-centered counterparts of the automobile or steel workers. This does not mean that powerful central offices in Paris control the behavior of the labor force. Not many workers belong to unions in the first place, there are several confederations which are as hostile to each other as to employers, and only one of them has much control over local unions. That one is the CGT *(Confédération Générale du Travail)*, which is the oldest and the largest of the national organizations. In 1945, after a quarter-century of struggle, it came under communist control.

In the period from its foundation up to the first world war, the CGT provided a center for the diverse tendencies in the labor movement, holding moderate reformers, anarchists, socialists, and syndicalists together in a most loosely organized coalition. The syndicalists in particular provided a flavor that made French unionism quite different from the central trend in the United States. (Much the same policies were represented by the IWW in this period in the United States, but the movement never had the importance here that it did in France.) Syndicalism favored worker control of production, eliminating both capitalist owners and the state. It joined the romantic strain of the anarchists, looking at union action "as a sort of dress rehearsal for the final climactic general strike. There was a strong stress on spontaneity, and it was not considered necessary that workers maintain a regular dues-paying relationship to the union as long as they would respond enthusiastically to strike calls."[2]

---

[2]James B. Carey *et al.*, "Trade Unions and Democracy," (Washington: National Planning Association, 1957), Pamphlet No. 100, p. 45.

For many years, and undoubtedly for some unionists today, "the fundamental law of French unionism,"[3] has been the declaration of principles approved by the CGT convention of 1906, called the Charter of Amiens.

> In its day-to-day demands, the union movement seeks the coordination of workers' efforts, the increase of workers' well-being by the achievement of immediate gains, such as the shortening of hours, the raising of wages, and so forth. This effort, however, is only one side of the work of the union movement. It prepares for the complete emancipation which can be achieved only by expropriating the capitalist class. It endorses the general strike as a means of action to that end. It holds that the trade union, which is today a fighting organization, will in the future be an organization for production and distribution, and the basis of social reorganization.[4]

The revolutionary phrases did not mean that French workers normally stuffed their lunch boxes with bombs. Latin languages lend themselves to dramatic statements, and the latter often serve as substitutes for action. At least up through the 1930's, labor disputes in the United States were more prone to lead to violence than labor disputes in France.

Nor did the obsession with social change lead the unions toward effective political action. In other industrialized countries of Western Europe, national labor unions formed close associations with the socialist parties and worked with them to achieve significant improvements in social legislation. In France, both anarchists and syndicalists were violently opposed to the idea of cooperation with any political party, and both were too strong within the CGT to permit any such political link.

Shortly after the First World War, the union movement split in three different directions. The Catholic Church had sponsored a group of unions which broadened their interests and reorganized in 1919 as the CFTC, the *Confédération Française des Travailleurs Chrétiens*. Within the CGT, the leadership decided to cooperate with the government in its reconstruction efforts, repudiating the joint opposition of communists, anarchists, and syndicalists. These groups attacked such cooperation as a betrayal of labor's class interests, and broke away to form a new national confederation. The separation provided an interesting test of worker preferences between the more pragmatic and the more radical concepts of unionism. Two-thirds of the CGT's members left it because of its turn away from the idea of class warfare.

The two wings of the CGT were drawn back on the same side in 1934,

---

[3]Léon Jouhaux, quoted in Henry W. Ehrmann, *French Labor, From Popular Front to Liberation* (New York: Oxford University Press, 1947), p. 21.

[4]From "The Charter of Amiens," quoted as appendix B in Val. R. Lorwin, *The French Labor Movement* (Cambridge, Massachusetts: Harvard University Press, 1954), pp. 312-13.

in opposition to attempts by right-wing extremists to overturn the government. Two years later, the communist-led confederation officially rejoined the CGT, accepting control by the socialists, in forming the Popular Front.

The victory of the Popular Front in the 1936 election touched off a contagion of apparently spontaneous strikes, in which workers in many industries took over plants and occupied them as if the old syndicalist dreams had come true. The strikes paralyzed the country in the weeks between the election and the transfer of power to the new government headed by Léon Blum. They created a climate of combat and crisis in which long-overdue reforms were quickly negotiated, but in which they appeared to industry as arbitrary dictations under extreme pressure. The sentiment of business leaders "was not that they had had to accept a new equilibrium of forces, but that their power had been profoundly shaken. They had lost face . . . ceded to illegal pressure, from fear of revolution."[5]

The *Matignon Agreements* forced through in these negotiations were quickly legislated by the new government. They established a 40-hour week and paid vacations of two weeks each year, required that shop stewards be appointed to channel worker grievances in large plants, and defined a complex process for identifying "representative organizations" with which employers could be compelled to bargain. Further, agreements negotiated in particular plants might under certain conditions be extended by law to cover other firms in the same industry or area. Arbitration procedures were established in a way that stopped short of compulsory decision by the government, but made it easy for either side to appeal to government arbitration. Too easy. Whichever side seemed to be losing promptly turned to the government, with the result that labor and business continued to avoid any real search for ways to negotiate successfully between themselves.[6]

In a real triumph of national traditions, the unions rejected the possibility of establishing regulations favorable to the closed shop or to the use of check-offs for more effective collection of dues. Both devices were considered by labor to infringe too severely on the rights of the individual worker.

The 40-hour week became the emotionally charged symbol of the whole set of reforms. It stood for much more than a mere reference point at which to begin calculation of overtime. Workers thought of it as a way of spreading jobs and thereby of reducing unemployment, but more fundamentally as an absolute limit on the time they would have to spend doing things under other people's orders. Employers thought of it as an unforgivable intrusion on the right of the firm to operate efficiently, an

---

[5]Jean-Daniel Reynaud, *Les Syndicats en France* (Paris: Armand Colin, 2nd ed., 1967), p. 88.

[6]See especially Ehrmann, *French Labor*, pp. 47-49.

increase in costs at a time when market conditions were highly unfavorable, and a grave handicap in the country's belated effort to rearm.

Within two years, as more conservative influences came back into play in the government, the 40-hour legislation was amended to encourage longer hours at nominal rather than penalty overtime rates. The following year, when the war started, the system was changed in a manner suggesting more a desire for revenge than a concern with production: workers were first required to work 45 hours weekly for the same total wage previously paid for 40 hours, then were allowed to earn overtime but only at a penalty rate below the standard for hours within the normal week.[7]

Although it was the 40-hour week that was most intensely debated, another aspect of the reforms was perhaps of greater potential importance. This was the idea of designating a representative organization for the workers in each plant or company, with which employers could be required to bargain. In the United States, this proved to be one of the key factors in developing more workable collective bargaining in the 1930's. The National Labor Relations Board certifies a single bargaining organization for workers in a given plant or craft category, and the union selected is then able to speak for the whole group of workers. This was apparently the original idea in France, but it foundered on a familiar rock. The Catholic unions would frequently come behind those of the CGT in any such voting process, and their members did not want to be represented by the CGT. So the practice adopted was to allow multiple representation. Competing unions within the same plant, with varying numbers of workers behind each of them, bargained for position against each other as much as against management.

Exactly the same problem recurred with postwar labor legislation. A new collective bargaining law adopted in 1950 contained the idea of selecting a representative organization, and met defeat for much the same reason. The CGT was still the largest group, and was by then under communist leadership. Members of the other confederations were not willing to let CGT unions speak for them, and the government had little wish to force them to do so. Consequently, multiple representation was accepted once again, and the system returned to the prewar difficulty. "Union rivalry at the conference table expressed itself in a series of competitive demands. Every union endeavored to demonstrate that its competitor was 'giving in' too readily to the employers, and the union representatives were reluctant to accept reasonable compromises out of fear of their rivals."[8]

Union positions in the period immediately after the Liberation were

---

[7]*Ibid.*, pp. 179-80.

[8]Adolf Sturmthal, ed., *Contemporary Collective Bargaining in Seven Countries* (Ithaca: Cornell University, 1957), p. 143.

powerfully affected by political considerations, first by the brief period of east-west cooperation, and then by the Cold War. Communist officials within the temporarily reunited CGT, strengthened by public identification with internal resistance to the Germans and by acceptance of communist membership in the government, emerged with key positions that enabled them to control the Confederation. When the Cold War split positions sharply apart again, the older reformist groups within the CGT, encouraged by American advisors, left it and founded the CGT-FO (Force Ouvrière).

Force Ouvrière has never been able to establish a strong position with production workers in manufacturing. It is particularly associated with white collar workers and civil servants. Its membership, like that of the other confederations, is difficult to count accurately. All of them tend to err on the generous side in stating their memberships, counting in workers who hold cards even if they do not participate in any way or even pay dues. It is generally believed that FO has less than half as many members as the CGT, and probably somewhat less than the other general confederation, known until recently as the CFTC.[9]

The CFTC was initially linked closely to the church, but became divided internally between those who wished to stay close to the original concept and those who wanted to make it less sectarian and more aggressive. The latter side gradually won out. In 1964, somewhat over 90 percent of its members voted to cut connections with the church and change the confederation's name to the CFDT, substituting "Democratic" for "Christian." The CFDT has since become the most active of all the confederations, making the CGT look strangely cautious and conservative in the strikes of May, 1968.

Total union membership has fluctuated widely, according to whether workers are awakened by a period of sharp controversy in which they seem able to play an important role, or are instead in a period of defeatism and generalized resentment. Membership went from about one and a half million in the early 1930's to six million with the advent of the Popular Front, then right back down again. It reached about six million once more shortly after the end of the war, but was probably back to two million before 1950. It stayed around that level most of the time until May, 1968, then jumped again in the enthusiasm of a period of successful action.

If the persistent core were taken to be two million, that would mean that about one wage or salary employee out of seven regularly belongs to a union. That is extremely low for industrialized countries in Europe, though not much lower than in the United States, where employees outside the industrial sector are not highly organized. In the metals indus-

---

[9]Reynaud, *op. cit.*, pp. 127-29.

tries, where organization is perhaps 80 percent complete in the United States, union membership in France is less than 20 percent.[10]

Negotiation Techniques and Strikes

It does not take complete organization for a union to have bargaining power. In most French industries, the test is whether or not the union can draw the unorganized workers into following them in specific disputes. And in some fields, particularly where government employees are involved, the degree of organization is high. This is particularly true of the coal mines, the maritime industry, ship construction, printing, railroads, teaching, and the civil service.

The type of strike most familiar in the United States—an indefinite withdrawal following a breakdown of negotiations on specific issues—is not at all common in France. In fact, it has a special name, *la grève illimitée*, to distinguish it from the kinds that the French usually think about. Those are two: nationwide general strikes, not focused on particular industries, and the short protest walkout for specified periods.

General strikes are relatively rare, even if one chooses to give that name to spontaneous breakdowns that sweep the country, as in 1936 and 1968, when workers explode and refuse to settle for anything less than major changes in national labor practices. This corresponds to the idea of the general strike, but it is noteworthy that these two spectacular revolts were not planned or called by the confederations. When they do call deliberate general strikes, as in 1939 and 1948, they are invariably unsuccessful.

By far the more common action is the one-day or even one-hour walkout. These manage to be most irritating, especially when they involve uncollected garbage or a paralysis of public transport. But they fall far short of the determined withdrawals that are characteristic of breakdowns in American labor negotiations. They reveal weakness rather than strength. They reflect lack of ability to make workers stay with a defined position, plus lack of union finances to help workers stay out until demands are met. Although strikes were common during the 1950's, man-days lost per worker averaged only one-third as high as in the United States.

Union dues are kept low partly because of a traditional belief that strikes should be financed through appeals to the public. Reliance on popular subscription rather than through coldly organized financial methods is intended to help "mobilize spirits." The CFDT created a furor in 1965 when its leaders opted for a more modern union with paid officials, and raised dues from 27 to 40 cents a month. Without much money, big strikes are limited to big occasions, and most have to be short. It is some-

---

[10] *Ibid*, p. 129.

times argued that this is a particularly potent strategy. Pulling part of a factory's workers out unexpectedly for 24 hours every once in a while creates the maximum of disruption per hour of pay lost, and is peculiarly hard on the nerves of management.[11] It would seem well calculated to keep relations as unpleasant as possible.

Both employers and unions have usually preferred to bargain for a region or nationally, rather than for one company at a time. In most industries, the employers' trade association, or a specialized labor relations association, represents all the companies jointly. The agreements typically specify minimum rather than actual wage rates, to avoid putting pressure on weaker firms while allowing others to set higher schedules at their discretion.

The main business federation, the CNPF, has moved a considerable distance away from the blindly anti-union positions of French industry in the prewar period. At least in principle, it favors the development of collective bargaining and of nationwide industry-labor agreements on such questions as supplementary unemployment insurance, or pay guarantees for temporary reductions of the working week. It may even intervene in labor disputes to put pressure on an individual company engaged in especially flagrant anti-union activities.[12]

Many of the larger corporations have, in varying degree, adjusted to reasonably orderly communication and negotiation with their workers and with unions. Collective bargaining developed very slowly in the 1950's but has gradually become much more common. The number of comprehensive agreements in effect increased by a fifth, and the total number of agreements including simple wage contracts increased by 40 percent, from October, 1963, to the beginning of 1968.[13]

The development of collective bargaining may have been stimulated by marked changes in techniques initiated by Renault in 1955 and again in 1962. The company's 1955 contract was patterned after settlements in the American automobile industry, and was intended to stimulate interest in single-company bargaining. It offered premia for expected productivity gains, a cost-of-living escalator, an extension of paid vacations from two to three weeks, and other modern trimmings then most uncommon in French negotiations. It was a very special case: Renault was trying to fulfill the expectation that a corporation owned by the government would lead the way toward better labor relations.[14]

---

[11]*Ibid.*, pp. 125, 142-54.

[12]Positions of the employers' associations are analyzed particularly well in Henry W. Ehrmann, *Organized Business in France* (Princeton University Press, 1957), and Reynaud, *op. cit.*, Chs. 2-3.

[13]Michel Despax, "Chronique des conventions collectives," *Droit social*, June, 1968, p. 387.

[14]J. Myon, "La Politique des relations sociales à la Régie Renault," in M. Boiteux *et al.*, *Le Fonctionnement des entreprises nationalisées en France*, (Paris: Dalloz, 1956), pp. 381-96; "Works Agreements of the Renault Type," *International Labour Review*, March, 1960, pp. 205-32.

Renault's example was followed by about fifty large firms in the course of the next two years, but most smaller companies continued to hold out for group negotiations. And the cost-of-living escalator was made illegal, three years later, on the ground that it aggravated inflation. The specific change that really caught on, and quickly became standard for all French industry, was the three-week paid vacation.

Although improved bargaining practices have gradually spread, a deeply ingrained sense of aggrieved paternalism still cripples negotiations of many firms. It comes as somewhat of a shock to read descriptions of company practices in the 1960's which include such statesmanlike devices as firing workers for leaving union folders in company dining rooms, assigning suspected organizers to isolated work in supply depots or on night shifts to break their contacts, refusing to allow union officials on company property, or even buying a field across from a plant to get rid of union signs posted where workers could see them.[15]

The right of union officials to contact workers on company property, for either information or collection of dues, and the right of union members to be protected from arbitrary discharge because of their membership, have been matters of bitter dispute throughout the postwar period. Until 1968, the law did little to support any possibility of union activity on company property, and not much more to protect members from arbitrary discharge. In principle, a worker fired for union activity could appeal to the *Inspection du Travail,* and the company could be required to pay compensation if it could not find some plausible reason for its decision. But the courts generally interpreted such protection to apply only to extremely clear-cut cases, and the company could not be required to reinstate the worker even then.

The relative lack of protection for workers has been related to a fundamental uncertainty about the degree to which economic policy has changed away from primary concern with sheltering inefficient producers. The companies that are the most belligerent in suppressing all signs of union activity are often weaker firms that might go under completely if they were forced to match the wages and working conditions offered by the more successful corporations. Not infrequently, they are the only firms in more backward areas of the country, taking maximum advantage of the lack of alternative local employment opportunities. In such cases, the government is clearly uncertain about whether or not the best policy is really to enforce laws on working conditions, or even payment of the legal minimum wage. "Two Frances exist, one where the respect of rules may be envisaged, the other, that of the underdeveloped regions where the fear of cracking a shaking structure leads the administration to tolerate breaking the law."[16]

---

[15]Herbert Ogrel, *Le Syndicat dans l'entreprise* (Paris: Éditions du Seuil, 1967).
[16]*Ibid.,* p. 20.

In the negotiations ending the nationwide strike of May, 1968, the labor confederations made a central issue of the right to contact workers within the plant and of accompanying protection for workers against dismissal for union activity. The employers' association accepted this position, and the government prepared new labor legislation to give force to the accord. The new law was passed almost unanimously at the end of 1968, underlining general agreement on the need for these changes. It would be surprising if all difficulties of implementing the intended protection were to disappear, but one highly promising aspect of the situation is that employers have not demonstrated any sign of the unyielding animosity with which they reacted to the similar national confrontation and changes in labor legislation resulting from the Matignon Agreement in 1936.

Wages

Although collective bargaining has been slow to develop, and unions have not been well organized or financed, something has worked: wages have gone up fast. As shown in Chart 1 on page 47, hourly wage rates in money terms have rarely increased less than 6 percent a year. In terms of purchasing power, deflated to adjust for increases in consumer prices, the increases have been more erratic. They averaged around 5 percent a year in the middle 1950's, suffered a sharp break in 1958–59, and then averaged 3.5 percent a year from 1960 to 1967.[17]

Wages have been pulled up by the need for workers in conditions of nearly continuous high employment, more than they have been pushed up by union pressures. But much depends on what period is considered. Important strikes in 1955 and 1968 certainly added to the rate of increase. And in quite a few years government intervention seems to have had significant effects.

Wages were officially set by the government until 1950, when collective bargaining was restored. A legal minimum wage, *le salaire minimum interprofessional garanti*, was introduced at the same time. This has been pegged to the cost of living in some periods, but cut loose and moved independently in others. From 1950 to 1955, as it proved difficult to develop general collective bargaining, the SMIG came to be taken as an automatic signal for adjustments of all wages. Whenever it was raised, employers moved up wages accordingly, no matter how far above the

---

[17]OECD, *Main Economic Indicators, 1957–1966*, pp. 207, 211, and July, 1968, p. 70. These figures refer to hourly wage rates, which are lower than actual earnings as measured by surveys of total "gains" by workers, but the long term growth rates of the two measures for all manufacturing are closely similar; cf. Marguerite Perrot, "Données statistiques sur l'évolution des remunerations salariales de 1938 à 1963," *Études et conjoncture*, August, 1965, pp. 37-39.

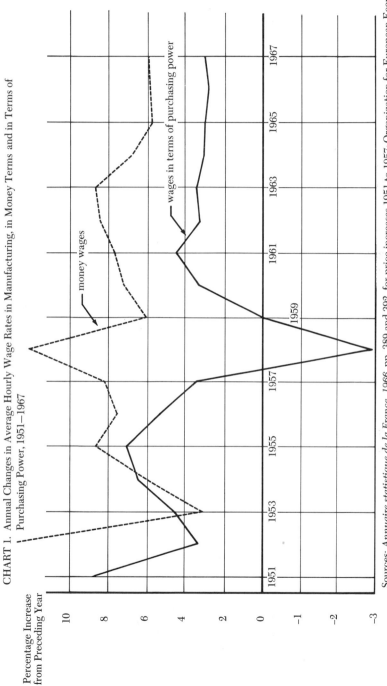

CHART 1. Annual Changes in Average Hourly Wage Rates in Manufacturing, in Money Terms and in Terms of Purchasing Power, 1951–1967

Percentage Increase from Preceding Year

money wages

wages in terms of purchasing power

Sources: *Annuaire statistique de la France, 1966*, pp. 389 and 392, for price increases 1951 to 1957; Organization for European Economic Cooperation, *General Statistics*, May, 1960 p. 75, for wages 1951 to 1957; Organization for Economic Cooperation and Development, *Main Economic Indicators*, for both wage and price changes from 1957 to 1967.

47

minimum. In 1955, after prolonged labor agitation in Nantes and Saint-Nazaire succeeded in forcing through a sharp increase in wages, this relationship was broken. Average hourly rates moved up much faster than the minimum wage from 1955 to 1968.

The government has returned frequently to efforts at wage restraint, with some periods of relative success. Premier Pinay negotiated an agreed slowdown as part of his campaign to stop inflation in 1952, and gained a sudden break from the previous rate of increase. Again in 1959, in connection with devaluation and accompanying policies to curb inflation, wages were held down severely; earnings in real terms did not rise for two years. After these controls were relaxed, wages went up rapidly until the stabilization program of 1963, which once more included direct wage restraints.

In all periods in which direct restrictions or negotiated wage slowdowns had some success, rising unemployment helped to reinforce their effects. This raises a difficult issue of interpretation: did the restraints actually work, or were they irrelevant because it was the increase in unemployment which held back wage rates? No one has carried out a conclusive study of the matter, but it should be noted that there is evidence of a fairly consistent statistical relationship between the number of people registered as unemployed and the rate of increase of wages, for the period from the end of the Korean War through 1967.[18] The relationship indicates that an annual rate of increase of wages equal to 6.7 percent a year corresponded to the average level of registered unemployed in this period, and that the rate of increase of wages could be expected to fall by 0.5 percentage points for an increase of 10 percent above that level of unemployment. There are many difficulties in interpreting any such relationship, and this one is at best a greatly oversimplified way to estimate what might have happened in the absence of direct restraints. But it does support the proposition that the generally low level of unemployment through the postwar period has been a powerful factor operating to raise wages, because it indicates that the rate of increase tends to speed up whenever unemployment falls. It also gives some modest support to the idea that Pinay's negotiated slowdown worked through 1953, because the actual wage rise in that year was distinctly less than would be predicted by the long term relationship between unemployment and wage increases.

In 1968, a nationwide strike succeeded in demonstrating that greater unemployment may not help to curb wage increases at all: with unemployment higher than ever, the strike settlement raised money wages more sharply than at any time since the Korean War.

---

[18]A simple regression of annual wage increases as a percentage of the preceding year (X_1), on the level of registered unemployed (X_2), gives the following relationship for the period 1953–67: $X_1 = 11.950 - 0.036\,X_2$. The computed t value for the regression coefficient
$$(0.011)$$
is 3.28. The adjusted r^2 is only 0.41.

From the workers' point of view, it has been necessary to raise wages rapidly because prices have gone up so fast as to undermine real earnings. At the same time, as in many other countries, the increases in wages have exceeded gains in productivity and helped make the price situation worse. Everyone could have been better off if slower increases in money wages could have been negotiated in return for correspondingly reduced price increases, but the society has not yet been able to accomplish the degree of cooperation that might make such a change in behavior possible.

Except for the interruption in 1958–59, there can be little question that real wage rates, in terms of purchasing power, have risen persistently. But it is true that they have not risen as fast as output per capita during the 1960's. The average rate of rise for real wages from 1960 to 1967 was 3.5 percent a year, and the rate of increase of gross national product per capita was above 3.9 percent.[19]

The structure of wages in France shows an interesting bias as compared to those of Germany and Italy. Real wages are in general higher in Germany and lower in Italy than they are in France, but in both cases nearly every industry has a higher ratio of costs for production workers, as compared to costs for salaried employees, than in the corresponding French industry.[20] That is, the ratio of earnings of salaried workers to hourly paid production workers is higher in France than in the other countries, whether the countries are above or below France in terms of productivity and average incomes. The discrepancy suggests that markets in the other countries have been better supplied with salaried employees; that France must have a relative shortage of educated white collar and technical workers. That in turn suggests that the society has not performed very well if it has a relative shortage of educated workers even as compared to countries with lower levels of income.

Considering three broad categories of employees—hourly paid production workers, salaried office employees, and higher level technical and managerial personnel (*cadres* in French classifications)—the highest paid group has gone up fastest in earnings since the war. For the period 1949–64, their earnings increased one-fifth faster than those of production workers. On the other hand, earnings of production workers increased slightly faster than those of salaried white collar employees below the *cadres*.[21]

Statistics on hourly wage rates for workers in different industries and with different skill classifications suggest a phenomenally rigid structure,

---

[19]The growth rate for GNP per capita is taken from OECD, *National Accounts of OECD Countries, 1957–1966* (Paris: OECD, 1968), p. 11, and *Rapport sur les comptes de la nation de l'année 1967* (Paris: Imprimerie Nationale, 1968), p. 137; but current revisions of the French national accounts indicate that they have underestimated growth in this period.

[20]A. Devaux, "Les Couts de main d'oeuvre dans les industries des pays du Marché Commun," *Études et conjoncture*, Feb. 1968, pp. 3-75.

[21]*Annuaire statistique de la France, 1966* (Paris: INSEE, 1966), p. 432 and facing chart.

as if all rates were determined by negotiations intended to keep relative wages exactly in line with each other.[22] But hourly rates do not take into account variations in fringe benefits, or the special premium rates that became important under conditions of full employment. A sample for metals workers in the Paris region in 1960 showed that average earnings ran up to 40 percent above agreed rates, depending on skill categories.[23] The premia rose systematically with the degree of skill, again suggesting the operation of market forces to adjust to a relative shortage of better trained workers.

Special bonuses and other fringe benefits make up a relatively high share of total wage costs for French industry. Workers do not, of course, object to fringe benefits. But they have opposed the spread of discretionary premia determined by the employer, as against standardized increases in basic rates. Special payments are believed to work in the direction of greater inequality (which is probably true), but above all to allow the employer to discriminate among workers in an arbitrary manner, and potentially to penalize those suspected of union activities.[24] Employers defend selective premia as a means of meeting competitive bids for particularly valuable workers, and for the positive effects on incentives they can offer. The conflict is familiar; what is different in France is that it has been resolved far more than in most other countries on the side of protecting the employer's right to unilateral determination, favoring incentives and flexibility at the cost of accentuating labor dissatisfaction.

Authority and Communication Within the Firm

The particular issue of discretionary premia would probably not seem so important if it were not caught up in a more general conflict over authority within the firm. More than in most industrial countries, labor seems to have held on to a traditional belief that the goal of organization is to enable workers to exercise control over industry. Similarly, more than seems to be true elsewhere, businessmen have clung to the belief that the slightest weakening in their authority will quickly lead to disaster. It is as if all decisions must come from the top down, to the point that even discussion of problems with union officials is regarded as a potentially fatal compromise.

The reluctance of management to conceive of any dilution of authority naturally varies with particular companies, and is perhaps less intense in

---

[22]Perrot, *op. cit.*, pp. 29 and 34; Jean Mouly, "Wage Determination: Institutional Aspects," *International Labour Review*, Nov. 1967, pp. 509-11.

[23]Arthur M. Ross, "Prosperity and Labor Relations in Western Europe: Italy and France," *International Labour Review*, Oct. 1962, p. 77.

[24]Cf. Ogrel, *op. cit.*, pp. 76-81 and 120; Pierre Le Brun, *Questions actuelles du syndicalisme* (Paris: Éditions du Seuil, 1965), p. 23.

larger corporations than in older family-run firms, but it is still remarkably strong in industry generally. It extends to suspicion and distrust of upper-level *cadres* as well as ordinary labor. The image of the modern corporation described by Galbraith—a "technostructure" in which technical and advisory personnel throughout the firm participate in formulating decisions which top management questions or accepts[25]—is scarcely applicable to the usual company in France. The image there is rather that of one man or a small group at the top, rather distrustful of any ideas that might come up from below, and greatly concerned with making it clear to everyone that authority is theirs alone.[26]

French Governments have frequently reacted to this situation by attempts to require that owners share control, or at least share their profits, with their workers. Such measures have been legislated repeatedly, from 1848 on through 1967. They have never had much effect.

Immediately after the war, the Provisional Government under de Gaulle tried several steps in the direction of giving workers a voice in formulation of company policies. For the newly nationalized industries, workers and consumer representatives were appointed to their boards of directors. For private firms, two kinds of consultative committees were required. All firms with ten or more employees had to establish "personnel delegates," to be elected by the workers and to meet regularly with management on working conditions. All those with over fifty employees were required to establish "plant committees" as well, to be given specific rights of access to company financial information and to present their positions on any and all aspects of company policy.

The committees called for by the law were simply ignored by management in some companies, and in general restricted to discussions of working conditions where they were allowed to play any role at all. In many cases they proved helpful in getting better safety protection, medical care, organized vacations for children of workers, and similarly humane improvements that employers did not always happen to volunteer. But decisions on pricing, investment, company finance, production change, and all the other vital questions that determine the survival and growth of the firm continued to be made by management, in the light of information and on the basis of criteria rarely made known in full either to worker representatives or to stockholders. This proved equally true of the plant committees and of the workers on the boards of the nationalized firms. How could it have been otherwise?

Legislation cannot change the need for a center of ultimate authority within the firm. It can conceivably do many things to guide the use of authority and to make it less arbitrary. As far as labor relations are con-

[25]John Kenneth Galbraith, *The New Industrial State* (Boston: Houghton-Mifflin Company, 1967), Chs. 6-8.

[26]François Bloch-Lainé, *Pour une réforme de l'entreprise* (Paris: Éditions du Seuil, 1963).

cerned, it can build up protection for workers and for unions. That side has been relatively neglected, but should improve with the new agreement and legislation of 1968. For questions concerning possibly antisocial use of company authority, it is always possible to enforce specific limits on behavior, such as rules of location, or for protection of the environment, or even restrictions on the right to change prices freely. Management authority can be made subject to external restraint without endangering efficiency, if the restraints themselves are reasonable and the firm is allowed freedom to act within known rules.

For the broader question often at issue in France, namely the choice of excessively authoritarian or secretive behavior that runs counter to efficiency and growth, there is a potential remedy which was long avoided but is now, somewhat haltingly, being applied: to encourage competitive pressures and let the misdirected companies disappear from the scene. One problem about this in recent years is that foreign firms have often appeared on the scene to take over the French company that has sunk into difficulties. The outstanding recent case, that of Citroën, was precisely that of a company with a long record of arbitrary anti-labor attitudes, secretive and extremely conservative management, and singular lack of. interest in developing exports. When it ran into increasing financial problems and Fiat tried to buy control, the French Government blocked the transaction and thus kept intact a management which has come to stand for much of what modern France has been trying to outgrow.

The preference for arranging new structures within firms by legislation seems to be at least temporarily suspended. The government gave much publicity to the idea that it was going to provide increased worker participation in management, during and immediately after the strikes of 1968, but business opposition plus a great deal of capital flight apparently led to second thoughts.

Another recurrent theme in efforts to lessen antagonism of workers toward management and toward the society has been the idea of generalized profit sharing. Decrees providing tax benefits to companies that would institute such plans were adopted in 1955 and 1959, but not many took advantage of them. The labor confederations did not exhibit much enthusiasm either, possibly because not much was done, possibly because of their traditional condemnation of profit per se, or possibly because they did not wish to pursue an experiment that might have had the ultimate effect of lessening the sense of class conflict.

With both sides reluctant to act, de Gaulle did. In 1967 he forced through a set of regulations requiring profit-sharing plans for all firms with more than one hundred employees. The theme of the law was that stockholders and workers should share 50–50 a specially defined *superprofit*. This refers to that part of profit, after taxes, which exceeds a return of 5 percent on the company's capital. Workers will not actually get the money for some time. It is to go into a fund, at the disposition of the firm, for a period of five years. Workers get interest, or dividends if their title comes in the form of stock holdings, and can take the principal out at the end of five years if it proves possible to arrange a payment or reinvestment scheme agreeable to both sides. If they cannot agree, the funds are tied up for eight years.

For the firms, the scheme has many complexities but little necessary cost. If the company chooses to increase investment by amounts equal to those put into the fund, it can deduct the whole payment from its tax bill. Amounts payable to stockholders would be reduced in the short run, but the firm would actually have more funds available for investment than it would in the absence of the scheme, and stockholders' equity would presumably grow faster because investment should rise.[27]

Current Strains and the Strikes of May, 1968

In the same year that the government created its complex and greatly watered-down scheme for enforced profit sharing, it decreed changes in the social security system reducing benefits and increasing taxes on workers, reduced the proportion of labor representation on regional boards administering social welfare programs, and decided to continue (through 1967) a restrictive set of monetary and fiscal policies that were raising unemployment to the highest level since the war. That did not prove to be a good set of policies to lessen worker antagonisms toward the rest of the society. In May, 1968, the country was paralyzed by the most impressive strikes of the whole postwar period.

The workers did not initiate the upheaval of 1968. It began with student demonstrations and occupation of the universities, more intense but similar to student revolts in the United States and elsewhere. France was the one country in which workers began to strike and occupy plants in sympathy with the students. The national labor confederations, much as in 1936, were confronted with spontaneous strikes all over the country. The force came from below and caught the leadership by surprise.

The confederations reacted in most interesting ways. Communist leaders in the CGT disavowed all talk of revolutionary overthrow and tried to channel the suddenly discovered bargaining power of their workers into demands for increased wages and reduced hours. They disassociated themselves as sharply as possible from the student revolutionaries, condemning them wholeheartedly for "leftist aberrations." The CFDT, on

---

[27]This may sound complicated, but it greatly oversimplifies the actual regulations. A summary of their effects published in *Le Monde* is headed: "as many cases as companies." (Selection Hebdomadaire, August 10-16, 1967), p. 9.

the other hand, tried to link workers with the students in demanding social change. They showed much less concern for mere wage increases, and much more for forcing through increased participation of workers in management of companies. They proved that the older national strand of syndicalism and drastic social reform is far from dead. The CGT, on the contrary, proved that a communist-led confederation can become a strong asset for a conservative government.[28]

In a manner highly reminiscent of the Matignon Agreement of 1936, the government brought the main labor and business leaders together with the Premier to negotiate a set of agreements for the whole country. The legal minimum wage was raised by a third, the general standard for wage rates other than the minimum was raised 10 percent, the employers' federation agreed to recognize the right of union members to engage in union activities on company property, and the government both raised unemployment insurance and retreated on some of the measures adopted the year before to reduce social security benefits.

Apart from the specific issues resolved, this form of labor negotiation at the highest national level, presenting individual companies and unions with prearranged norms of settlement, tends to enforce rigid patterns irrespective of local conditions or questions of allocative efficiency. The negative effects may be reduced by a good deal of outright non-compliance, but this does not seem to be either an efficient or an attractive solution. The alternative would be to strengthen bargaining processes at the individual company level, a process which has been under way but has probably been set back by the government's own highly centralized approach to all such problems.

In 1968, the government set a splendid example for the most recalcitrant employers. When the radio and television broadcasters of the government-owned system joined the strikes in May (asking for the right to greater independence in news presentation, rather than for increased wages), the government simply refused to negotiate the main requests at issue. The broadcasters eventually gave up, after assurances that participation in the strike would not be held against them. The government then announced a reorganization of news services that ended the jobs of most of the people identified with leadership of the strike.

Centralized, political-style, labor negotiations seem inescapable if labor has no real voice in the normal formulation of government policy. With the main labor confederation under communist leadership, with a high

---

[28]Of the many books on issues involved in the May upheaval, two particularly useful interpretations are: Club Jean Moulin, *Que faire de la révolution de mai* (Paris: Éditions du Seuil, 1968), and Raymond Aron, *La Révolution introuvable* (Paris: Librairie Arthème Fayard, 1968).

proportion of the urban labor force voting communist no matter what the issues or whom the candidates involved in elections, and with communists excluded from the government, it is almost as if workers were disenfranchised. To revise the social security system in the process of labor negotiations seems an absurdity, but it was perhaps the only answer to a government which had changed the system in 1967 by decree, without any apparent interest in public discussion. Labor negotiations in France are too political, but this is perhaps inevitable as long as the political process itself is not genuinely representative.

Social Welfare   **5**

An exuberant burst of generosity at the end of the war gave France an exceptionally thorough welfare program, suddenly changing the country in this respect from one of the most backward of all the industrialized nations to one of the most advanced. Assistance provided for individual problems of health and medical care, maternity and family benefits, unemployment compensation and retirement pensions, went at least as far as, and in some respects beyond, the "welfare state" introduced in England at the same time.

Generosity is one of the few characteristics of human beings that make the species seem, at times, to be worth preserving. It can also be a very complicated business. Nothing comes free, and costs which are not foreseen have a way of undermining or even reversing intended benefits. A large scale program of social welfare can easily go astray either by placing the costs on the people it is intended to help or by running against incentives to raise efficiency and production. The French system has been criticized on both counts. It is true that it has landed much of the cost on the same social groups that receive the benefits. But it can hardly be considered to have had any grievous effects on efficiency; the record of economic growth in the period since it has been adopted is probably the best in all French history.

Social welfare legislation offering significant help to particular groups had been adopted before the war, and had been extended to all lower-wage industrial workers in 1930. In 1944, the National Council of the Resistance spelled out a much larger objective for the postwar world. Their goal was to ensure comprehensive coverage for everyone in the society against all the uncertainties of health, unemployment, personal disability, or unacceptably low incomes from whatever cause. This *Resistance Charter* was approved by all political parties immediately after the war, and provided the framework for the welfare system adopted by the Provisional Government in October, 1945.[1]

One of the objectives of the system as originally intended was to provide equal benefits to all, regardless of differences in ability of individuals or groups to contribute to its financing. It was a plan to redistribute income in the process of providing equal benefits, rather than an insurance scheme allowing greater benefits in relation to contributions. This side of the program ran into too much opposition to be implemented fully, and has gradually been given less and less emphasis. Those groups receiving special benefits through separate welfare systems previously established or created at the time of the nationalizations, held on to the right to stay apart from the central system. And higher-salaried *cadres* led a successful effort to generalize supplementary welfare programs, in which they make greater contributions in order to receive greater benefits. The coverage of the central *régime général* has been persistently extended, but the differential schemes have been maintained and probably increased in relative importance.[2]

Social Welfare payments to households have risen faster than national income all through the postwar period. As of 1967, they were equal to 22 percent of disposable income. This was two and a half times as high as the corresponding ratio in the United States in the same year.

Family Allowances

Family allowances are a standard feature of social welfare systems in European countries, though nowhere so fully developed as in France. The French pioneered their adoption before the war, and provided unusually high levels of support immediately after the war. The program has two purposes. One is the wish to help families with children in order to lessen inequalities of real income, much as the American exemptions for children in the income tax system are intended to do. The second purpose in France is quite different: it is, or at least it was when the original high level of supports was established, to encourage larger families.

As a measure of income equalization, family allowances are clearly

---

[1]Wallace C. Peterson, *The Welfare State in France* (Lincoln, Nebraska: University of Nebraska Press, 1960), Ch. 2.

[2]Jean Moitrier, "Y á-t-il un plan français de sécurité sociale?" *Revue économique*, March, 1967, pp. 177-204.

TABLE 1.   Social Security Payments in Relation to
Disposable Income of Households in 1967

	Million francs	Percentage of disposable income
Retirement pensions	37,007	9.7
Medical, maternity, and death benefits	23,513	6.2
Family allowances	17,508	4.6
Accidents at work	4,534	1.2
Unemployment benefits	252	0.1
Total	82,814	21.7

Source: Ministère de l'Économie et des Finances, *Rapport sur les comptes de la nation de l'année 1967*, (Paris: Imprimerie Nationale, 1968), pp. 44 and 142.

superior to the use of exemptions from income taxes. They give great help to families whose incomes are too low to be subject to taxes at all, and therefore who get no benefit from exemptions. They also give equal help to equally sized families regardless of income levels, whereas the system of personal exemptions gives the greatest benefit to those whose incomes and marginal tax rates are highest. The French make sure by approaching the objective from both angles. Besides the direct payments, they allow an extended form of family tax splitting. Where the American system allows husbands and wives who use joint returns to reduce tax rates by splitting the family income in two, the French method allows splitting for children as well, with each child counted as one-half. A family with two children can split its income in three for tax calculations.

Direct payments are of two kinds. One is related to the number of children. It allows nothing for the first child, 22 percent of a standard reference wage for the second, and 33 percent of the same standard for each additional child. This payment is kept up through age fifteen or beyond that for the minority of cases in which the child's education continues. The standard used has been raised more slowly than actual wage rates, so the relative importance of the benefits has gradually decreased. The other type of payment is an allowance for families in which only one parent is employed. In 1957, the two types of payment combined averaged 29 percent of wages-plus-benefits for workers' families with three children.[3] For those in lower-wage occupations, the allowances were of course even more important.

Policies which encourage larger families may seem odd in a world properly concerned with population pressure acting to hold down living standards. Overpopulation is a critical problem in many low-income countries, and rapid population growth imposes strains in any country, however rich. But public opinion in France is still strongly influenced by

[3] J. Hochard, *Aspects économiques des prestations familiales* (Paris: Union National des Caisses d'Allocations Familiales, 1961), p. 121.

a half-century of failure to grow at all, with the dismal thought that something must be extremely wrong with a country in which people had so little enthusiasm about the future that families were not on balance reproducing themselves.

In the first few postwar years, the French birth rate went way up, just as it did all over the world. The rate in France went up to 21 per thousand for the period 1946–50, below that in the United States but still the highest rate for any major West European country, and much above the average of 15 per thousand experienced in France in 1935–37. When the birth rate came down in other industrial countries during the 1950's, it did the same in France, falling to 19 for 1951-55, 18.2 for 1955–60, and 17.8 for 1960–66. Total population has grown fairly steadily at an annual rate of 1 percent. The population was forty-one million in 1946, exactly the same as it had been within the same territory in 1901; it reached fifty million in 1968.

The introduction of family benefits coincided with the end of a century-old downtrend in birth rates. So did the end of the war, a change to high employment and general prosperity, and many other conceivably relevant factors. It is impossible to be sure either that the policy contributed to the change in behavior or that it did not. It seems reasonable to assume, since it reduced the economic risks and costs to the family of having children, that it did help keep postwar birth rates higher than they would otherwise have been. At any rate, the assumption that they did so is appealing: it would suggest that societies can to some degrees control their own fates in this important area by selecting policies which point in the direction that the country wants to go.

Family benefit payments have remained a relatively stable proportion of national income since the late 1940's, while the number of children covered within the system has approximately doubled. That is, the payments per child have fallen greatly in importance relative to direct earnings. This probably reflects a lessened sense of concern now that a moderate rate of population growth seems to be an established behavioral pattern. It also reflects rising costs of other social welfare programs, notably that for health insurance.

Medical Benefits

Expenditures under the health insurance program increased from 1.5 percent of national income in 1949 to 2.5 percent in 1960 and 5.8 in 1967.[4] By 1967, the government decided that the costs of this system

---

[4]Pierre Grandjeat, *La Santé gratuite* (Paris: Editions du Seuil, 1965, p. 14; *Comptes de la nation, 1967*, p. 142. The data refer to *prestations en nature* (payments for medical care), not including compensation paid for loss of earnings.

were rising too rapidly, and adopted some acutely controversial measures to restrain them.

One of the causes of increasing cost is that the coverage of the program has been progressively extended. As of 1958, 66 percent of the population was covered; by 1962, this had risen to 86 percent.[5] The major change in this period was the inclusion of farm families. The only groups that remain without coverage are storekeepers and those who either never were able to work or were retired before being covered by the insurance system. The retired who are not in the insurance system are protected by the older institution of free medical care for needy cases: their medical coverage is generally good, though their pension support is poor.

A second factor involved in rising expenditures is the cost of medical services. As in the United States, this has gone up faster than the general price level. The fundamental cause is similar: pressure of rising demand on a field in which trained personal services are crucial, and equipment increasingly complex. There is an important difference on the French side. That deep-seated fear of the American Medical Association, that the government may become directly involved in fixing doctors' fees, is a reality in France.

The insurance system provided for a method of negotiating standard fees between regional medical groups and health insurance officials, with the government to set the fees where negotiations broke down. They broke down badly in the high-income areas. A strike by the doctors helped force a more generous system of fixing and moving the standards for fees in 1960, and led to a new method allowing individuals to join the system even where the regional association voted against it.[6] Four out of five doctors have now joined, but the proportions in Paris and Lyons remain much lower than this.

It would not help a great deal to finance medical services for more and more people if the ability to take care of them were not raised correspondingly; it could do considerable harm if efforts to hold down charges for medical services worked out to drive people away from the profession. But the restriction of fees has not so far had any such negative effect. From 1952 to 1965, the number of doctors increased at an annual rate of 3.2 percent. The total number of people involved in the provision of health services, including nurses, dentists, and laboratory assistants, has increased at an annual rate of about 4 percent. The growth rate for the whole set of professions involved in health services has been approxi-

---

[5]Grandjeat, *op. cit.*, p. 27. The measure of coverage includes both the central *régime général* and the various special programs providing slightly different forms of protection for particular groups.

[6]Henry Rosen, "La Santé" in Pierre Laroque et al, *Succès et faiblessess de l'effort social français* (Paris: Armand Colin, 1961), pp. 83-84.

mately the same as that in the United States during the postwar years; that for doctors alone has been far greater than in the United States.[7]

A third important reason for the rise in health insurance expenditures is that the French people have responded to the program with an enthusiastic increase in the amount of medical care they want to have. The trend shows no signs of slowing up: an investigating commission forecast a growth rate of 7.6 percent a year for an index of all forms of medical care, at constant prices, for the period 1960–1970. The fastest increases in the past have been for drugs, hospitalization, and laboratory analysis. In a period in which the method of payment of doctors remained stable, from 1957 to 1960, the annual number of doctor visits per person for people covered by the general insurance system increased at a rate of 4 percent a year. From 1960 to 1963, after a revision increasing the effective rate of reimbursement for consultations, the number of visits grew at an annual rate of 10 percent. Farm families, under a separate program, were still required to pay the first one hundred francs ($21) of their medical bills in 1962; this fee was eliminated in January, 1963, and doctor consultations for these families increased 73 percent over the level of 1962.[8] This is what the system is for. Medical care expenditures by farm families had been far below those of urban workers. Giving them similar access to insurance coverage helped them to catch up, just as the general program has had the effect of allowing lower income people to raise their health standards toward levels previously possible only for the wealthy.

While there can be little question that health insurance has opened access to medical care on more equal terms for nearly everyone, there may easily be question about the total cost. This has been debated chiefly in terms of financing for the insurance system, which has been in deficit. It goes well beyond that issue, to the question of the objectives of the society.

The health insurance system, like that for family benefits and pensions, has been financed in principle by payroll taxes. As in the United States, these taxes have been varied in two dimensions: in terms of the base salary to which they are applied, and in terms of the percentage of tax against the base. As expenditures have increased, both the base subject to tax and the rates used have been steadily raised. The wages included in the taxable base are lower than in the United States (Up to 1140 francs a month in 1967, about $230). The tax rates are high; 28.5 percent for employers, and 6 percent for workers until the revision in 1967. These

---

[7]*Annuaire statistique de la France,* 1952, p. 41, and 1967, p. 101 *Cinquième Plan de développment économique et social,* tome II, p. 16; Rashi Fein, *The Doctor Shortage* (Washington, D.C.: The Brookings Institution, 1967), pp. 66 and 114. The number of doctors in the U. S. increased at a rate of 1.9 percent a year from 1949 to 1962.

[8]Grandjeat, *op cit.,* pp. 31, 37.

changes increased the employee's tax to 6.5 percent, and added a new wrinkle. Workers now must pay an additional 1 percent, and employers 2 percent, on all salaries in excess of the base amount.

The deficit of the welfare system was growing so fast that these additional taxes, and administrative revisions to take certain charges off the social security accounts, were not expected to do more than to reduce the 1968 deficit by about a third. The other two-thirds are supposed to be taken care of by an increase in the proportion of medical bills which individuals must pay themselves.

The method of handling most medical costs has been to let the individual make his own arrangements and payments, then to reimburse the expenditures. For somewhat over half of all expenditures, the reimbursement is not complete. It covers the actual total less a percentage known as the *moderating ticket*. The percentage reimbursed by the government has varied for different types of expenditures. In general, operations and long hospital stays presumed to be essential (and not things that people would be expected to undergo excessively just because they were free), were compensated fully. Doctor's bills have been compensated at 80 percent of the standard rates fixed for the particular service; if individuals choose to go to doctors charging more than the standard, they are stuck with the extra costs. Costs of drugs have been reimbursed 70 percent.

In 1967, the government increased the moderating ticket for doctor's services, reducing reimbursement to 70 percent of costs. This was presented explicitly as a means to limit the growth of demand for medical care. The government made it clear that further steps in the same direction would be taken if the deterrent did not prove sufficient, and even proposed to outlaw any private or cooperative insurance scheme that would have the effect of covering completely the marginal costs of additional medical care. The change became one of the more bitterly disputed issues of economic policy in the period immediately preceding the nationwide strikes of 1968. The labor confederations made it a central point in the negotiations that helped to end those strikes; the government retreated half-way, setting the reimbursement rate at 75 percent.

The idea of limiting the growth of demand to fit the rate at which the supply of medical services can be increased has, of course, a highly logical basis. If something of great personal importance cannot be made available in sufficient degree to meet everyone's wants, which is and probably always will be true of medical care, then people should be discouraged from wasting it for marginal concerns. The method chosen to discourage trivial claims on scarce ability to provide medical care is classic; everyone will have to pay a higher percentage of his own bill. The difficulty with this solution is classic too. The deterrent will have no effect on the degree of recourse to medical care by the wealthy, though it may lead poor people to postpone requests for help with serious problems.

Effects on Costs and Incentives

The other side of the 1967 revisions, the increase in payroll taxes to support health insurance, has the effect of shifting the burden from the general tax system to a tax on wages. It acts to raise labor costs and prices. The main "tax" which pays for the welfare system is a higher level of prices of commodities. In a general sense, people must consume fewer goods if they wish to consume more medical services. But the financing method is probably regressive, because people with higher incomes spend a lower proportion of them on consumer goods than poorer people need to.

Although the costs of the welfare system are directed disproportionately toward lower-income people, so are the benefits. This is true especially for the benefits provided to the retired and disabled. Despite the relatively regressive method of financing, the system as a whole certainly does have some modest effect in changing the distribution of real income from higher to lower income groups, and from the active population (both wage earners and self-employed), toward the inactive disabled and retired.[9]

That last statement may sound ominous. The welfare program favors the inactive at the expense of those contributing to output. An economic system which works on the basis of incentives could easily run into trouble if non-functional income became too important relative to earned income. But French experience so far, with transfers over twice as high in relative importance as they are in the United States, has not indicated any serious weakening of incentives. With a 40-hour work week as the reference point beyond which further work is more-or-less voluntary overtime, the actual average work week has been persistently around forty-seven hours. A higher proportion of adult women choose to work in France than in the United States. Flexibility among regions and jobs, traditionally very low in France, has improved in the postwar period. Labor has usually seemed scarce, but that is because demand has been strong, not because people do not want to work. And demand has been so strong because investment and the rate of growth have been kept high. The economy has certainly not been paralyzed.

The welfare program has been criticized for raising prices and making it more difficult for French firms to compete in export markets. This is sometimes stated as if the program were outrightly inflationary, because expenditures have outrun the payroll taxes earmarked for them. That need not be the case at all. Adequate general taxation, holding aggregate demand within the limits of capacity to produce for the economy as a whole, would limit inflation no matter what deficit were involved in the welfare system considered separately. But it is probably true that rising payroll taxes act to increase product prices, and French payroll taxes on

---

[9]Cf. Peterson, *The Welfare State in France*, Ch. 4.

employers are certainly steep. They could seriously hamper exports, and ability to compete with imports, if they made French prices rise faster than those in other countries. That is, they would do so unless the exchange rate were adjusted to correct the situation.

No country need suffer any competitive disability, no matter how high the monetary charges of its welfare system, if it chooses the correct exchange rate to go with them. When the franc was devalued at the end of 1958, this placed French industry in a strong competitive position, taxes and all. But if a country freezes the exchange rate and goes on increasing payroll taxes, as France has been doing in the last several years, it will get into trouble. The objective of remaining competitive would seem to call for the same financing method as would a concern for equality in income distribution: less reliance on payroll taxes and more on income taxes.

Social Investment and Education

While the French made a great step forward in the provision of social welfare support through income transfers, direct investment in facilities to provide better living conditions lagged far behind. The first postwar plans stressed industrial investment to the point of attempting to discourage housing investment, despite the country's ferocious housing shortage. Relatively little attention was given to building or improving hospitals, to urban renewal, or to provision of better facilities for education. In 1962, the first year of the Fourth Plan, total social investment expenditures were less than one sixth as much as transfer expenditures. They were equal to 1.6 percent of gross national product.[10]

The Fourth Plan, starting in 1962, was the first one to direct attention to this lag and give priority to efforts to correct it. The plan projected an increase of 50 percent in total social investment in four years, compared to expected increases of 28 percent for investment in directly productive economic activities and 24 percent in total output. Increases in both public and private consumption were to be held below the rate of growth of production in order to release resources for both public and private investment.[11] The results did not match all the targets—public consumption in particular grew much faster than expected, while research expenditures reached only 80 percent of the objective—but total social investment came close to the mark, increasing 48 percent in terms of constant prices.

---

[10]*Rapport sur les comptes de la nation de l'année 1966,* pp. 45, 361, and 489. Social investment as intended here does not include road construction; it is the total for education and research, public health, and "collective equipment," both rural and urban; *ibid.*, p. 45.

[11]Bernard Cazes, *La Planification en France et le IV Plan* (Paris: Éditions de l'Épargne, 1962), p. 117.

The Fifth Plan altered targets slightly, reducing that for social investment relative to private capital formation, but not by much. The ratio
of intended growth rates for the two categories of resource use was 1.79
in the Fourth Plan and 1.68 in the Fifth. The Fifth Plan put special
emphasis on research and on secondary and higher education, two areas
in which France's performance seemed to be particularly far behind
immediate needs.[12]

Provision of greater financial support for education was clearly over-
due, even though it could be no more than a partial answer to the many
difficulties of the educational system. These problems center on obstacles
to social integration, but they also bear in crucial ways on the function-
ing of the economy. French educational methods have always been extraordinarily effective in conveying and enriching cultural traditions, but
singularly ineffective in creating the conditions necessary for a flexible,
decentralized society. That is to say, they accomplish exceedingly well
what they were designed to do, but that does not seem to be what is
needed if the society wishes widespread economic opportunity and rapidly
growing incomes.

The main structural characteristics of the educational system were
established in the Napoleonic Period, and built in so strongly that they
have survived countless reforms. They emphasize the selection of a small
elite to provide leadership through centralized direction. The great
majority, those who are not among the chosen, are given formalized in-
struction fitting them for specialized tasks but not for the exercise of
initiative or participation in decision making.[13]

One of the great strengths of the Napoleonic system has been that it
applies severe tests of ability in the selection of leaders. On the negative
side, it applies these tests only to people who have been pre-selected by
a discriminatory social process. Students in primary school have been
divided very early between those who indicate interest and aptitude for
the classical subjects considered central to a genuine education, and those
whose interests or capacities go in other directions. Those children whose
family backgrounds were not such as to foster concern for Latin or
classical philosophy were almost automatically excluded from the channels
leading on to higher education. And once the child was placed on a given
track, crossing over was next to impossible. Children given more vocational
types of training because they are expected to stop at the compulsory

---

[12]*Cinquième Plan de développement économique et social* (Paris Imprimerie des Journaux
Officiels, 1966), tome II, pp. 35-64 and 293-312.

[13]Cf. Michel Crozier, *The Bureaucratic Phenomenon* (Chicago: University of Chicago
Press, 1964), pp. 238-44; Robert Gilpin, *France in the Age of the Scientific State* (Princeton
University Press, 1968), Ch. 4; Michel Morisot, "L'Enseignement," in Pierre Laroque, et al.,
Succès et faiblesses de l'effort social français (Paris: Colin, 1961), pp. 141-65.

minimum age of fourteen, arrive at that point in a poor position to recon-
sider the matter. Not surprisingly, the proportion of children from families of urban workers or farmers who go on to higher education has been
persistently low. In 1962–63, children of families in the liberal professions
or upper management had forty-two times as great a probability of going
to a university as children of working class families.[14]

For those who do complete secondary school successfully, entrance
into the best institutions of higher education, the *grandes écoles*, has
depended on rigorously competitive examinations. The process screens
out mediocrities very well. It then stamps the successful few (about 4
percent of the total going on to higher education) as the official adminis-
trators of the country's institutions. By assuring them that they can remain
for life in key positions, and by assuring everyone else from an early
stage that they are not expected to enter such positions, the system
assures a minimum of personal mobility. It has strongly supported centralized decision making and maintained a sharp cleavage between the
few at the top and the many who could not get there.

All through the postwar period, imaginative people concerned with
the rigidities of the educational system have been working on possible
ways to improve it. Many reforms have been adopted. They have gone
some way toward loosening the structure of differentiation in the early
grades, increasing the possibilities of crossing over between programs, and
opening up wider opportunities to go on to higher education.[15] Progress
in these directions was real and important, but limited by two constraints:
great resistance by many of those brought up under older methods and
opposed to change, and lack of money to implement new programs once
approved.

National expenditures on education are closely related to levels of
income. Compared to poorer countries, French expenditures on education
are high; compared to the United States they are low. One interesting
attempt to establish a systematic relationship between income per capita
and educational expenditures per capita, for twenty-three countries as of
1960, suggests that France was moderately below the normal relationship.
Income per capita was about on a par with Denmark, Norway, Germany,
and the United Kingdom, but educational expenditures per capita were
lower than in any of them. Of all twenty-three countries, France was
10th in income per capita, 13th in educational expenditure per capita,
and 15th in educational expenditure as a percentage of national income.
On the other hand, the rate of *increase* in the percentage of national

---

[14]Pierre Bourdieu et Jean-Claude Passeron, *Les Héritiers* (Paris: Les Éditions de Minuit,
1964), p. 15.

[15]Morisot, *loc. cit.*; John Ardagh, *The New French Revolution* (London: Secker and Warburg, 1968), Ch. 10.

income devoted to education between 1950 and 1960 was fifth highest.[16] France must have been extremely far behind as of 1950, but then began to catch up. Similarly, new entrants to universities as a percentage of their age group increased rapidly. It was only 4.6 percent in 1950, but 9.1 percent by 1959 and 12.2 percent by 1963. For 1963, that ratio was the highest in Europe.[17]

The rapid increase in numbers of university students during the postwar period was one of the most important accomplishments of the society, but it raised rather than eased tensions focused on the educational system. Restricted budgets and totally inadequate attention to improvement of facilities led to extreme overcrowding and extension to the point of caricature of mass lectures, to the exclusion of anything resembling student-teacher exchange of ideas. The clear-cut distinction between education for the ordinary university student, and a privileged track for the small group in the *grandes écoles*, was kept carefully intact. Decisions on salaries, appointments to particular universities, examination methods, and all the details of administration in every university, continued to be made on a completely standardized basis by government officials in the Ministry of Education, rather than in the schools.

From about 1965 onward, a new source of strain made things worse: as the growth of the economy slowed down and unemployment began to increase, it became increasingly difficult for university students to find jobs in the fields for which they had been trained. Since university education is highly specialized in content, as well as relatively inflexible in method, graduates who found no openings in the fields for which they were prepared also found themselves unable to turn in new directions other than at relatively low levels of rank and pay. That new worry may have been the final reason for the force behind the student revolt of May, 1968. That explosion shut down the country's universities completely, led to nationwide strikes and to serious question of the ability of the government itself to survive, and then to a most promising set of reforms. They suggest considerable decentralization of the university system, greater flexibility in secondary school education, and increased participation by students in decisions affecting them. They do not alter the preferential character of the *grandes écoles*, and they abstain carefully from promoting any form of competition among the universities to build leadership in specialties or to pioneer methods differing from each other. But they mark a clear step forward, and seem to be supported by greatly increased

---

[16]F. Edding, "Expenditure on Education: Statistics and Comments," in E.A.G. Robinson and J.E. Vaizey, eds., *The Economics of Education* (New York: St. Martin's Press, Inc., 1966) pp. 39-41.

[17]K. Eide, "Educational Developments and Economic Growth in OECO Member Countries," *loc. cit.* p. 181.

willingness to provide funds as needed to catch up on provision of facilities and teaching staffs.

Improvement of education, public health facilities, cities and rural areas—the collective facilities essential to a decent society—requires human initiative and imagination more than it requires money, but it requires money too. Postwar French programs channeled a great increase in financing through the social welfare systems, but left social investment behind. The balance in recent years seems to be going in the other direction: transfer expenditures keep growing, but educational and other social investment is now growing faster.

Planning 6

French planning aims at guiding the economy toward consciously selected goals without giving up private ownership of the means of production or the right to independent choice in individual markets. It is not an authoritarian system, but one of the more successful of the modern hybrids: it is based on group consultation within a framework intended to ensure consistency, backed up by incentives for cooperative action.

The idea of a national economic plan comes readily where cultural traditions favor the visibly systematic mind rather than the invisible hand. Pierre Massé, the director of the Planning Commission from 1959 to 1965, explains planning in the same terms as rational human activity: *"une aventure calculée, une lutte entre le hasard et l'anti hasard . . . [Les plans], sous les formes les plus diverses, ont pour contenu commun la conscience et l'intentionalité, opposées aux fatalités et aux hasards."*[1]

The Early Plans: Modernization of Industry

During the 1930's there were many proposals for adoption of an economic plan, coming from widely different political groups. The Popular

---

[1]Massé, *Le Plan ou l'anti-hasard* (Paris: Gallimard, 1965), p. 7. Approximate translation: human activity is "a calculated adventure, a struggle between chance and anti-chance . . . . What plans have in common, under their varied forms, is consciousness and intention, opposed to fate and to chance."

Front government considered the idea seriously in 1936 but finally decided against it. It came back again as one of the goals of the Resistance movement during the war, preparing the way for favorable action by the first postwar government.

The initial plan was intended to guide postwar reconstruction, worked out partly to support requests for American aid. The man who initiated the program, Jean Monnet, designed it for much more than mere repair of war damage. For the industries chosen for immediate attention, production and investment targets were set in terms of a high rate of economic expansion. Management was brought into a series of discussions with the planning agency, and told in some cases to change their investment choices to prepare for a greater scale of production. The program was conceived and sold as an attack on restrictionist thinking; an attempt to reorient the attitudes of French producers, both industrial and agricultural, from acceptance of stagnation toward the idea of sustained expansion.

The initial program covered the period 1947-50, later extended to 1952 to fit the timing of the Marshall Plan. It would probably fail to meet any of the standard criteria used by the people concerned with planning in so many of the developing countries today. It did not rely on use of overall national accounts, or include any thorough analysis of balance among sectors. It was simply a set of action programs for a few particular industries. Initially, they included coal, electric power, transportation, steel, cement, and farm equipment. As the programs got under way in these fields, the Planning Commission went to work on other industries considered to be both important and lagging in the process of reconstruction. The emphasis was not on orderly sequence and overall consistency; it was on pushing things into motion.

The content of the system differed among fields, and has since differed considerably with the passage of time. The original approach can perhaps best be indicated by comparing the treatments of electric power and steel.

With the nationalization of all private power plants, the industry had become a single firm, the *Électricité de France*. In the first instance, the only step that the Planning Commission took with respect to the EDF was to specify a goal for electric power capacity far higher than prewar peak. The director of the EDF stated later that the objective amazed the officials of the agency and caused them to raise their sights. A few years later, it looked too low.

The EDF was left largely on its own to prepare its investment program to meet the stipulated target, and its proposals were readily approved. But by 1950 it began to seem doubtful that the approach was working well. One difficulty was that the EDF opted whenever possible for large-scale, capital-intensive, hydroelectric power projects, as opposed to steam plants or simpler hydroelectric installations. Their preferred type of project offered considerable savings in current operations, at the cost of higher initial investment outlay. Since the EDF was carrying out an essential program approved by the Planning Commission, it was given ready access to credit at low interest rates. This stacked the cards artificially in favor of capital-intensive methods, at a time of severe capital shortage and inflation.

The Commission reacted by requesting the EDF to prepare alternative investment packages. This made it possible to rank programs, and in the process to put the more capital-expensive projects last. The debate led both sides to sharpen their techniques of project analysis, and eventually to the adoption of useful guides to decision. The Commission began to specify the interest rate which the nationalized firms were to use in all their investment calculations, and set it at levels above those the firms actually had to pay for borrowing. The economic concept of opportunity cost of capital, as distinct from the actual rate of interest paid, began to be used systematically in the selection and design of projects.

When dealing with the EDF, the nationalized railroad system, or the coal mining industry, the Planning Commission remained in the role of providing generalized guidance. It did not get involved in questions of management or industry organization. But its approach to planning in the steel industry, in the first period, was quite different. It was a thorough attempt to remake the structure of the industry.

As discussed in Chapter 2, the Planning Commission rejected the steel industry's own reconstruction program. The Commission's program called for greater concentration of new investment in favorable regions, encouraged new combinations of firms to centralize production on a larger scale, and specified that the industry should establish two jointly-owned new plants to catch up with modern technology. None of this constituted an absolute order to the industry to do things it did not wish: some of the firms were themselves interested in carrying out these steps, and others were encouraged to cooperate by being given preferred access to credit for the recommended investment projects. The Planning Commission probably came as close to giving outright orders in this case as it ever has, but the main reliance was, even then, on persuasion and inducement. The program was worked out with the industry, and the relative profitability of cooperation was raised by the offer of special finance, but firms which wanted to ignore it remained free to do so.

In its subsequent dealings with this and other industries, the Planning Commission has been much more circumspect about anything resembling directives to management. It has often suggested consideration of changes in the balance of total of industry investment plans and offered help with financing for action on the lines suggested, but financial aid is often forthcoming even when the industry does not fully accept such suggestions. The Commission has promoted particular mergers and tried to influence decisions on location of new plants, but in the great majority of cases it simply takes as given the basic structure of the industry.

The formal approach to industry planning has remained close to the original idea of joint industry-government consultation. The Planning Commission prides itself on operating with a small staff, able to follow the main problems of each industry but not expected to draw up detailed programs on its own. The Commission starts things going about three years ahead of the time a plan is intended to go into effect, with a broadly defined set of major options and themes to guide discussions. The main step in designing the industry plan comes through consultation in working groups which bring together delegates from the industry, from suppliers and customers, and from interested government agencies.[2]

Delegates to the working groups are chosen by the Commission. They are usually picked from the larger firms whose decisions are considered to count most heavily, rather than with any attempt to ensure balanced representation. In a few cases, the trade association is regarded as sufficiently dynamic to be acceptable as the main channel for negotiation. Where the association represents numerically dominant smaller firms the Commission does its best to keep the organization out of the picture.

The delegate of the Commission in these working groups is in a position to provide useful information about the probable evolution of markets and supply availabilities, to make suggestions on the basis of continuous observation of the industry, and to offer support on financing or on discussions within the government on policy matters of interest to the industry. If the firms concerned have made up their minds on what they want to do and have developed their own financing capacities adequately, they can simply go ahead without worrying about contrary advice.

Explanations of the process by the people from the Commission itself put considerable weight on the fact that they can provide firms with projections of the probable evolution of markets. In principle, if all firms used these projections for their own investment planning, they would simultaneously make the plan come out right in total and make the industry's investment come out right in terms of markets. This neat picture is clouded by the fact that the Commission's projections do not have any impressive record for accuracy. Some industries have successfully increased and sold output at growth rates more than double those

[2]Cf. Pierre Bauchet, *Economic Planning, the French Experience* (London: Heinemann, 1964);

Bernard Cazes, "French Planning" in Bert G. Hickman, ed. *Quantitative Planning of Economic Policy* (Washington, D.C.: The Brookings Institution, 1965), pp. 179-211;

John and Anne-Marie Hackett, *Economic Planning in France* (Cambridge, Mass.; Harvard University Press, 1963).

projected as targets, and others have not found it possible or desirable to raise production by more than a small fraction of the projected rate.[3] At the start of the Second Plan the Commission succeeded in getting the steel industry to reduce its plans for expansion, arguing that they would lead to excess capacity; three years later the country ran into a serious shortage of steel and was forced to turn to imports on a large scale to alleviate supply bottlenecks.

The natural reply to the forecasting problem is that the numerical projections are not what count anyway. The planners "had always been concerned with the growth of the productive power and efficiency of French industry; output and investment figures included in the plan had merely been used as a means of attaining the more profound purpose."[4]

If the goal were to hit the numerical targets, the method would have to be more authoritarian. As it is, much of the strength of French planning has come from the modesty of the degree of pressure applied, which leaves firms free to follow their own preferences and to take advantage of new openings not foreseen or foreseeable in the plans. For example, suppose that the automobile industry and the refrigerator industry were both given reasonably established targets of expanding output 8 percent per year, but that consumer preferences changed so that demand for automobiles increased by twice that rate and demand for refrigerators did not grow at all. If the targets in the plans were followed rigidly, there would be a growing shortage of automobiles and excess capacity in refrigerators; both industries would contribute more to the country's welfare if they ignored the plans and moved with consumer preferences. Very fortunately, firms are not forced to follow the predetermined target. "It is the great virtue of French planning that it has left individual firms free to experiment, innovate, overexpand and underexpand by restricting its planning to indications rather than commands."[5]

The original Planning Commission, under Monnet, had a strongly expansionary bias. Whatever output targets might have seemed reasonable in terms of previous experience, they raised. Reacting to the historical record of near-stagnation, their overriding objective was to stimulate action breaking through old restraints, without much concern for conflicting claims on resources. This is easier to do when dealing with a few specific industries than when operating on the whole economy. Industries compete with each other for scarce inputs, and get in each other's way if

[3]Cf. especially Andrew Shonfield, *Modern Capitalism* (New York and London: Oxford University Press, 1965), pp. 134-37.

[4]*Ibid.*, p. 141.

[5]Charles P. Kindleberger, "French Planning," in National Bureau of Economic Research, *National Economic Planning* (New York, NBER, 1967), p. 288.

they all try to expand faster than total resource availabilities allow. The Commission gradually began to give more attention to analysis of overall resource use, and to explicit policy choice for the economy as a whole. Industry planning continued, but it gradually became of decreasing importance relative to questions such as the desired balance between private and social consumption, and the pattern of growth of money incomes.

The Recent Plans: Social Goals and Overall Policies

To some degree with the Third Plan, and much more fully with the preparation of the Fourth (for 1962–65), concern for broad options of economic policy became the main feature of the plans.[6] Concern for detailed industry planning gave way to greater emphasis on questions of the uses to be made of gains in production. The Fourth Plan no longer focused on industrial investment; it gave first priority to raising investment in schools, hospitals, communications and transport.

The intent of the Fourth Plan was to maintain such a high rate of aggregate expansion that social expenditures, both for investment and current transfers, could be stepped up greatly without slowing down industrial investment or private consumption. The scheme was heroic but it did not work out neatly. Wages and prices went up rapidly. In 1963, the Ministry of Finance outvoted the plan. A stabilization program was introduced that applied monetary and fiscal deflation to slow down demand. As explained in Chapter 8, the stabilization program worked well and did not seriously slow up growth until after the end of the Fourth Plan, but it did emphasize greater concern about price stability and contributed to the choice of a slower growth rate for the Fifth Plan.

The Fifth Plan (for 1965–70), maintained priority for social investment, though its intended rate of growth was reduced slightly relative to that for industrial investment. Since the expected rate of growth of total output was reduced, retention of rapid growth rates for both forms of investment meant that consumption had to be slowed down. The plan called for greater restraint on private consumption and for brakes on the rate of growth of social welfare expenditures.

To support the intended changes in the pattern of resource use, the Fifth Plan introduced specific guidelines for rates of increase of particular forms of income. These were calculated to be consistent with price increases at a rate of 2 percent a year, considered to be safe enough for the purpose of meeting international competition. But even without going so far as to program for complete stabilization of prices, the plan implied

---

[6] Cf. Geoffrey Denton, Murray Forsyth, and Malcolm Maclennan, *Economic Planning and Policies in Britain, France and Germany* (London: Allen and Unwin, 1968), Ch. 3.

distinctly changed behavior for wages. Compared to a 6.9 percent annual rate of increase in wages and salaries from 1960 to 1965, the plan allowed for a rate of 5.0 percent from 1965 to 1970. The expected rate of gain in real wages per worker was reduced to 3.3 percent per year, compared to 4.9 percent for the period 1960–65. The rate of gain of real income per capita in agriculture was planned to go in the opposite direction: up from 2.5 to 4.8 percent per year. In line with the goal of continuously rising investment, corporate saving was projected to increase by 6.4 percent a year, as against 4.4 percent for the period 1960–65.[7]

The expression of the plan in terms of values and corresponding flows of money incomes was meant to clarify possibilities, not to provide directives. Massé did organize a conference including labor and business representatives to present and discuss the idea of collectively negotiated agreements on income flows, but was not supported by either side.[8] Labor spokesmen, with the exception of the CFDT, opposed the principle as a subterfuge for wage controls. Business representatives recoiled from any suggestion that they should discuss desirable rates of profit with either the government or the unions.

In the absence of any agreement that might limit the growth of money incomes at full employment, consistent with sufficient restraint on prices, the Fifth Plan build in a deliberate projection of rising unemployment. That is, the projected growth rate was too low, given expected increases in productivity, to provide enough new employment opportunities to match the growth of the labor force.

The plan itself does not, of course, cause any particular growth rate or level of employment to occur. But it did serve as a signal for the general line of government policies. Monetary and fiscal deflation were carried on into the period of the Fifth Plan, despite rising unemployment, and the government adopted new measures to curb the rate of growth of social welfare transfers. This should not be taken to mean that the plan compelled the government to take this particular course of action. It was rather the other way around: the government used the plan to express its policies.

The Planning Commission has never been in any position to dominate the government's economic policy; it is simply one influence within a complex set of interests. In the early postwar years, it benefited from the fact that many other agencies of government shared concern for the same objectives of modernization and increased investment. In the last

[7]*Cinquième Plan du développement économique et social* (1966–1970), Paris, 1965, Vol. 1, Tables 22–24, pp. 189-91.

[8]"Rapport sur la politique des revenus établi a la suite de la Conference des Revenus," presented by Pierre Massé (La Documentation Française, 1964); John Sheahan, *The Wage-Price Guideposts* (Washington, D.C.: The Brookings Institution, 1967), pp. 113-16.

decade, its support has been less consistent, and its own independence probably decreased. The Commission did not favor, but was unable to prevent, either the devaluation of 1958 or the stabilization program of 1963. Since the departure of Massé in 1965, the directors appointed to run the Commission seem to have been less interested in exerting independent influence intended to change the direction of economic policy. The present government does not encourage discordant voices from within its own ranks.

Apart from questions of negotiating positions among government agencies, the economic environment has been changed in ways that make the power of the Planning Commission distinctly less than before. The banking system has been greatly liberalized, lessening specific restraints on investment that is not associated with plans. And the reduction of trade barriers has made it more difficult than ever to project accurately the evolution of either individual markets or the whole economy. Furthermore, it has made it more essential than ever that producers emphasize reduction of costs and selective growth on lines of greatest relative efficiency, which are not the kinds of choices easily made by a central agency concerned with aggregative growth.

In this new context, planning has retreated from specification of detailed goals, or from deliberate restraint of particular fields. The retreat has been subject to a great deal of criticism by those who believe that firm direction of choices is necessary to guide the economy to preferred goals.[9] The argument usually comes down to a statement of the necessity for positive social choice in the methods of accomplishing major structural adjustments, such as the transformation of agriculture, correction of the housing shortage, or renewal of cities. And in those areas it is surely correct. Social welfare and major structural transformations require conscious decision, and the decisions can be made more efficiently if the society has before it a relatively clear picture of the implications of alternative choices for the economy as a whole.

Planning can be a great help in illuminating the consequences of policy alternatives such as price or income support to farmers, subsidies for construction of low-cost homes, or many of the other selective actions by which governments try to promote the goals of the society. But redirection of resource use in such areas can be accomplished by budgetary decisions and allocation of contracts through open market procedures; they do not require extensive use of specific production targets and differential aids or handicaps to alter behavior of individual producers.

---

[9]Jean Bénard gives a well balanced and particularly clear, but despairing, statement of this position in "Le Marché Commun européen et l'avenir de la planification française," *Révue économique*, Sept., 1964, pp. 756-84. See also Claude Gruson, *Origine et espoirs de la planification française* (Paris: Dunod, 1968).

French planners have always had power to influence behavior through selective incentives. If the power were great enough, it could come close to outright compulsion. In the period of the First Plan, the pressures were relatively strong. Since then, and especially in the 1960's, the development and liberalization of the credit system have combined with explicit preferences of the Planning Commission to lessen reliance on use of differential incentives to induce specified behavior for particular industries. French planning is still more than merely suggestive; it does try to alter incentives, but it is far removed from the use of pressures so strong that they amount to orders.

Democratic Control

The process of planning raises important political questions. At one extreme, if the legislature were free to change any items in the plans, the coherence of the system would be destroyed. At the other, if only the planners had the skill and information needed to work out the implications of each choice, if the package had to be regarded as unalterable, there would be no scope for democratic political choice.

In the French case, the issue was initially solved by default. The Planning Commission went ahead as it intended, and submitted the plans to Parliament for ratification rather than for debate, sometimes well after the plans were in operation. "In some ways, the development of French planning in the 1950's can be viewed as an act of voluntary collusion between senior civil servants and the senior managers of big business. The politicians and the representatives of organized labour were both largely passed by."[10] The procedure might be defended on the ground that it worked in the public interest, or that the decidedly unequal representation of private interests in the planning process was not much more biased than that in the political system itself. It could be defended, and it worked, but it was not a satisfactory process in a country which values democratic methods.

External review of the plans was initially made the responsibility of the Economic and Social Council. The Council, established in 1924, is composed of representatives of a wide range of interest groups, including labor, private employers and nationalized firms, agriculture, independent professionals, and even "non-representative intellectuals with special competence in economics or science."[11] The Council does not constitute part of the legislative process; its recommendations carry some weight in Parliamentary debates, but more particularly they serve to give guidance

---

[10]Shonfield, *op. cit.*, p. 128.
[11]John and Anne-Marie Hackett, *op. cit.*, p. 51.

for the government in formulation of proposed legislation. It provides a forum for consultation among economic interest groups, and has permitted helpful discussion of the sense of the plans. But it was not able to apply the close and continuous supervision of detailed choices which would have been necessary to affect their content in any significant way. The Commission did nothing to help, at least during the first three plans: it presented them as final packages, not subject to tampering.

Beginning with the Fourth Plan, the Commission made a greater effort to present the plans as embodying the consequences of a set of *grandes options*, which the Council and Parliament could meaningfully debate prior to final formulation. For the Fourth Plan, the options presented did not go very far: they essentially consisted of three different possible growth rates, with a predetermined package of programs attached to each. In preparation for the Fifth Plan, the Commission presented instead a set of issues, facilitating debate on the degree of priority to be attached to social investment, agricultural incomes, military expenditures, aid to developing countries, and business self-financing for investment. At the same time, the Commission tried to limit the range of debate by projection of a ceiling on supply availabilities, subject to the priority requirement of increased investment.

The debates that surrounded the Fifth Plan turned out to be of great interest as a test of possible reconciliation between popular control and professional expertise in economic planning. The labor representatives in the Economic and Social Council tried to overcome the restrictions specified by the Commission, arguing that greater output should be possible and that less industrial investment would be needed. They were outvoted by business and government representatives, possibly just for reasons of political preference, but possibly also because the more socially-oriented choices seemed to violate resource constraints calculated by the professionals concerned with planning.

In a sense, positions remained doctrinaire and it was simply the set of relative weights in the voting process that made the result a victory for acceptance of resource constraints. But that was not the whole consequence. Labor leaders, who have so often disdained specific technical questions in their concern for pure ideological positions, joined with economists to study in detail the technical validity of the plan. They prepared an alternative, internally consistent, and much more expansionary *contra-plan*. They were able to show fairly convincingly that the official program implied significantly rising unemployment, beyond anything made clear in the plan itself.[12] The debates did not change greatly the content

---

[12]Julien Ensemble (pseudonym), *Le Contra-Plan* (Paris: Éditions du Seuil, 1965); Pierre Le Brun, *Questions actuelles du syndicalisme* (Paris: Éditions du Seuil, 1965), pp. 155-63.

of the plan, but they did serve to bring labor leaders into confrontation with economic constraints, into meaningful examination of rational possibilities as a background for choice.

During the height of the demonstrations against the government in May, 1968, at a mass reunion led by students in the Charléty Stadium, the banners included the slogan, *"Contre le V$^{i\grave{e}me}$ Plan."* That must have been painful to Jean Monnet. Planning began as an ideal of reawakening the economy, providing new opportunity, and building a better future for France. But that was a generation ago. Now planning and a vigorous economy are fairly well taken for granted. And planning has become partially identified with deals favorable to business as well as, in the case of the Fifth Plan, with deliberately increased unemployment and restraints on the achievement of social objectives.

The reaction against it by labor and by the young is understandable, and to some extent well founded. Planning can become a most conservative instrument of policy, if it is controlled by people primarily concerned with conservative objectives. It need not go that way. It can open the way to more fruitful confrontation between goals and possibilities for the whole society, and could easily be brought back in this direction by a government concerned with democratic processes as well as economic efficiency.

Monetary Management and The Tax Structure

7

Monetary and fiscal techniques provide powerful ways of favoring particular policy objectives and holding back competing claims on resources. In the United States and many other countries, use of this power is carefully limited to avoid altering incentives or giving favors to particular groups. The one systematically intended departure from that general neutrality is the effort, in the federal tax system, to place a relatively greater tax burden on people with higher incomes. In France, the basic presumptions have in some respects been the contrary. Monetary and tax incentives have been used aggressively to encourage particular lines of investment. Tax burdens have not been directed to higher income groups, but rather to consumption in general, in order to release resources for investment. The main objective has not been to preserve neutrality, but to foster a high rate of growth and to guide resource use deliberately.

The Monetary System

Prior to the Second World War, the French monetary system was less subject to centralized control than the American. There was no close equivalent to the Federal Reserve. The Bank of France had many of the characteristics of a central bank, under a system of contractual relations with the government, but it was privately owned, competed for ordinary

83

commercial business, and lacked authority (until 1938) to take initiative in open market operations. Its relationship to other banks was more that of a competitor than a supervisor or lender of last resort.

At the end of the war, one of the major objectives of economic reform was to establish public control of the flow of credit, to assure financing for the investment programs approved in the plans and to eliminate what was considered to be an area of private privilege. The Bank of France, several insurance companies, and the four largest deposit banks were all taken over by the government.[1] A new board, the National Credit Council, was established to determine monetary policy for both the government-owned and the private banks.

In addition to the newly nationalized banks, the government owns several other monetary institutions originally established to handle specialized functions. The largest of these is the *Caisse Nationale des Dépôts et Consignations*, which dates from the early nineteenth century. It receives and invests funds coming into postal savings accounts, handles the funds of local governments, the pension funds of nationalized corporations, and other special accounts outside of the regular banking system.[2] After the war, the flow of finance through this institution rose greatly and its policies changed markedly. Instead of directing its funds primarily to government securities, it took an active role in providing long-term financing for investment by local communities, low-cost housing, and industrial investment. It became an important source of finance for both government agencies and private firms whose investment programs were approved by the Planning Commission. The *Caisse* formed an integral part of the planning process.

Much the same process occurred with another government-owned financial institution, the *Crédit National*. This bank had been established after the First World War to aid in reconstruction. After the Second War, it came to serve as a key source of medium-term finance on a selective basis.

Business requests for investment financing above stated amounts could not be granted by any bank without prior approval of the Planning Commission. With such approval, the *Crédit National* would assure automatic discounting privileges, so banks could undertake medium-term

---

[1]The "deposit banks" are approximately similar to American commercial banks, except that they are allowed more freedom in security dealings. Cf. Holger L. Engberg, "French Money and Capital Markets and Monetary Management," *The Bulletin* of the New York University Graduate School of Business Administration, Jan.-March, 1965; J.S.G. Wilson, *French Banking Structure and Credit Policy* (Cambridge, Mass.: Harvard University Press, 1957), Chs. 2 and 3.

[2]Jean-Pierre Gaullier, *Le Système bancaire français.* (Paris: Presses Universitaires de France, 1967), pp. 55-67; Andrew Shonfield, *Modern Capitalism* (New York and London: Oxford University Press, 1965), pp. 167-169.

loans with no fear of any liquidity problem. Approved investment could also be financed from a special fund for modernization and equipment, initially supported from the counterpart of American aid, or by the *Caisse des Dépôts*. The directors of both the *Caisse* and the *Crédit National* cooperated closely with the Planning Commission to make sure that investments in accordance with the plans could be financed on favorable terms. For the investment programs of government agencies, the *Caisse* provided a source of finance outside the regular budgetary process, increasing their freedom to carry out long-term plans. Neither of these institutions were new, or were in any way subject to direct control by the Planning Commission, but in both cases the postwar plans provided a focus transforming their traditional functions and linking them to a central program directed at wider goals.[3]

Centralized guidance of the monetary system was provided by the National Credit Council, with authority over public and private banks alike. The Council has been likened to the Open Market Committee of the Federal Reserve.[4] There are some similarities, including the fact that the Bank of France provides the staff work for the Council, so that it almost forms part of the central bank. Although the official chairman of the Council is the Minister of Finance, the real director is the Governor of the Bank of France. But, in contrast to practice within the Federal Reserve System, the Council includes representatives of executive agencies of the government, business groups, and even labor unions. It is somewhat as if the Open Market Committee were officially led by the Secretary of the Treasury, and included such people as the Chairman of the Council of Economic Advisers and the Director of the Bureau of the Budget, plus representatives of the NAM and the AFL-CIO.

Whether it is to be explained by the character of the National Credit Council, or more fundamentally by the preferences of the country, French monetary management from 1945 to 1963 was distinguished by its heroic ability to rise above any obsession with deflation. The money supply was regularly allowed to increase rapidly enough to keep up with a fast rate of economic growth. All parties concerned resisted any temptation to prove that they could stop price increases by stopping the economy.

In the immediate postwar years, there was little attempt to set any quantitative limit to bank lending. The emphasis was entirely on qualitative controls. Banks were advised to favor loans for investment on the part of industries designated by the economic plan, and to resist loan requests for doubtful purposes such as inventory accumulation. In some periods, they were advised to restrict lending to particular industries con-

---

[3]See especially Andrew Shonfield, *op. cit.*, pp. 166-71.

[4]Engberg, *op. cit.*, p. 53.

sidered less essential, such as food processing, leather, and textiles. The deposit banks were required to observe established liquidity ratios, but these did not have the same meaning as in the United States. They were meant to ensure solvency, not to control lending power. Unlike American practice, the banks were expected to be normally in debt to the central bank and could easily get more reserves by rediscounting.

In principle, each bank had a specified ceiling for the amount of rediscounting it could request, plus a floor of required holdings of short-term Treasury securities. But the limit on rediscounting was usually not applied restrictively. Banks could go above their individual ceilings, at the price of penalty rates, and the ceilings themselves were often raised when they seemed to be restricting lending activities.

Recent Changes in Monetary Techniques

Priority for expansion of public investment and approved plans was maintained even during the efforts of the Pinay Government to stop inflation in the early 1950's, and during the radical changes in economic policy initiated under the Fifth Republic at the end of the decade. But the latter changes did have important consequences for monetary techniques and objectives. They were generally aimed at reducing specific intervention to control the structure of the economy. Credit policy shifted more toward quantitative limits on the whole money supply, and restrictions on bank lending for particular industries were gradually eliminated. Lending on favorable terms to industries with approved investment plans continued, but access to credit for purposes outside the plans improved.

Beginning in 1961, a new system gradually cut down on the open-ended character of loans for approved investment programs. The former floor for holdings of government securities by banks was replaced by an effective reserve requirement. Banks were required to hold freely discountable paper in a minimum ratio (originally 30 percent) to their deposits. This meant that loans which previously could have been rediscounted outside the credit ceilings now had to be held, up to the specified ratio, by the bank itself. And the ratio soon began to move up.[5]

Once the method of control shifted toward overall restrictions on credit extension, as opposed to exemptions or negotiated compromises for specific types of loans, the French system began to lose much of its discriminatory character. Approved investments connected with the plans may still entitle firms to loans at lower rates of interest, but the selective barriers for loans not so approved have largely been removed. And banks themselves have been allowed much greater freedom in their activities. The old distinction between deposit banks and investment banks has

[5]Engberg, *op. cit.*, pp. 58-60.

largely been removed, with all of them permitted an almost unrestricted range of investment activities. In this sector, perhaps more than any other, the experience with selective restraints and detailed rules of bank conduct seems to have led to a pronounced preference for a more liberal system.

The reduction of selective direction has been criticized for weakening the power of the plans to guide investment choices. There is no doubt that it weakened any power the Planning Commission had to block investment of which it disapproved. That power was used in the earlier postwar years to slow up investment by consumer goods industries and, briefly, to restrain investment in housing. But it has not since been an essential part of the Commission's operations, nor congenial to its other policies. Its main source of pressure has been the offer of low-cost loans and special tax incentives for particular projects it supports, not the negative weapon of blocking access to ordinary credit for projects it does not support. The positive weapons are still there.

The Tax Structure

While monetary management has changed in ways that have made it more like our own, the structure of taxation has remained markedly different. It remains primarily an instrument of selective direction, supporting investment and exports while trying to hold back the growth of consumption.

In the early postwar years, taxation was too confused to serve as a positive instrument of any clear economic policy. A high proportion of revenue came from turnover taxes applied at every point of sale. Their effects cumulated erratically, depending on the number of transactions involved in the production and distribution process of a given product. They encouraged excessive vertical integration, weakening incentives for firms to gain efficiency through specialization. Income taxes were used also, but they were flagrantly evaded. Small business in the more backward sectors of the economy, small retailers everywhere, and independent professionals as well, were renowned for their successful evasion. Farmers hardly paid any taxes at all, though that was more by virtue of intentionally favorable methods of assessment than because of any special recourse to fraud.

Tax evasion is more difficult in the better organized sectors of the economy. Profits of corporations and wages of their workers are relatively easy to verify. But that means that the burden of income taxation lands unfairly on the more progressive, growth-oriented sectors of business, and on their employees. Successive governments have tried to correct this bias by more accurate taxation of earnings in the rest of the economy, but have been defeated by a fundamental obstacle: most people regard evasion as legitimate. A survey of public opinion concluded that 59 percent of the country's businessmen and 61 percent of professional people approve of it.[6]

Tax verification squads were organized in the early 1950's and proved that they could be effective, but were stopped by the Poujadist revolt. The government tried to insist, but gave up when Poujade, a small storekeeper in a particularly low-income region, began to run candidates for office on a simple program of denouncing taxes, captured strong support in the region, and won 52 seats in the National Assembly elections of 1956.[7] In the most recent attempt to tighten taxes at the retail level, when extending the tax on value added to this sector in 1968, the government finally backed down from its proposal to apply the same tax in all retail stores, and allowed the smaller ones to continue with a method that is much lighter for sellers who maintain high margins.[8]

Postwar tax reform has minimized reliance on income taxes, recognizing their inequity under present conditions, and emphasized improvement of indirect taxes instead. The most important by far, pioneered by the French and adopted as a model for tax revision in the rest of the Common Market, is the tax on value added. This was applied to industry in 1954 and has now been extended to agriculture and to commerce. It far outweighs income and corporate profits taxes combined. It is a much more rational system than the turnover taxes it replaced, with interesting connotations for resource use and income distribution.

The tax is imposed on the value of a firm's production, minus the cost of the inputs purchased for production. It is administered as a tax on sales, from which the company can deduct a credit for similar taxes included in the prices of its purchased materials. As compared to a tax on profits, it has a broader base: it includes profits, but also wage costs, charges to reserves, rent, and interest. It is not applied to capital goods or to exports, only to goods going to domestic consumption. The net effect on production methods is to make capital goods cheaper relative to labor than they would otherwise be, and thus to encourage investment and labor-saving. Similarly, by shifting the tax burden from capital goods toward consumer goods, it hits consumers and makes it possible

---

[6]Pierre Tabatoni, citing Jean Dubergé, in National Bureau of Economic Research and Brookings Institution Conference Volume, *Foreign Tax Policies and Economic Growth* (New York: NBER, 1966), p. 292.

[7]Jean Rivoli (pseudonym), *Vive l'impôt!* (Paris: Éditions du Seuil, 1965), pp. 13-17.

[8]John Ardagh, *The New French Revolution* (London: Secker and Warburg, 1968), pp. 109-10.

to apply lighter taxation to the higher income groups and corporations which do most of the saving.[9]

The tax on value added does have one feature that works in the direction of greater equality. The rates applied to food products are relatively low, and those applied to luxury goods are above average. It may thus be moderately progressive as compared to a flat tax on consumption, though it is surely less so than most systems of income taxation. The differential rates suggest that the purpose is not to establish a regressive system, but more specifically to hold back consumption in order to favor investment.

Corporate profits are taxed at rates slightly above those in the United States (50 percent, as against 48 percent here), but this tax has less meaning than it does here. High depreciation rates and multiple deductions for incentives act to hold down the value of what is considered profit. General depreciation rules were revised in 1959 to make them more favorable to investment for all firms, and special exemptions have been developed in negotiations with particular firms and industries. The steel producers were allowed to charge depreciation in proportion to sales to encourage investment in cooperation with the plans, exporters have been permitted extra depreciation based on the proportions of their total sales which are exported, approved individual corporations which sell new stock have been allowed to deduct dividend payments as if they were interest costs, special write-offs are permitted for investment in less developed areas of the country and for reconversion of firms required to adjust to competition in the Common Market, and so on almost indefinitely. The deductions permitted are so generous "that the share of corporate income deductible as depreciation (nearly 50 percent) was far higher in France than in the United States, Great Britain, Sweden, Japan, or Canada."[10]

Such extensive recourse to special exemptions has several important consequences. In the first place, it helps to stimulate exports and investment. In the second place, it directs more of the tax burden to households and consumption. Thirdly, within the business sector itself, it favors particularly the larger and better organized corporations which are best placed to realize, or to initiate, opportunities to get special treatment. None of these consequences is unintended. They all fit a central policy

[9]Otto Eckstein and Vito Tanzi, "Comparison of European and United States Tax Structures and Growth Implications," in National Bureau of Economic Research and Brookings Institution Conference, *The Role of Direct and Indirect Taxes in the Federal Revenue System* (Princeton University Press, 1964), pp. 247-48.

[10]Martin Norr and Pierre Kerlan, *Taxation in France* (Chicago: Commerce Clearing House, 1966), p. 105. Exemptions are detailed in this study, pp. 666-700, and in Tabatoni, *op. cit.*, pp. 275-329.

preference for growth, and a presumption that the forces for growth are best embodied in the largest corporations. It should perhaps be noted that many of the corporations in question are owned by the government. But that does not seem to be a significant question in this context: the point is to promote large corporations, no matter whether privately or publicly owned. The method does not do much to foster the emergence of new firms, or the growth of that fraction of smaller business which may be oriented in useful directions that have not happened to catch the attention of promotional agencies.[11]

TABLE 2.   Main Sources of Current Government Revenue in France, Germany, the United Kingdom, and the United States, 1966

Percentage distribution of current revenue [a]

	France	Germany	United Kingdom	United States
Direct taxes on households				
Social security	36.7	27.5	14.0	17.9
Other (chiefly income taxes)	11.6	22.4	28.4	34.4
Direct taxes on corporations	4.9	6.1	7.5	16.2
Indirect taxes (on sales and value added)	45.1	38.4	43.6	31.5
Governmental profit and entrepreneurial income	1.3	5.0	6.7	(b)

Source: Organization for Economic Cooperation and Development, *National Accounts of OECD Countries, 1957–1966,* (Paris: OECD, 1968), pp. 48, 124, 136, 280. Reference is to all levels of government, not to central governments alone.
Notes: (a) Percentages need not add to one hundred because current transfer from the rest of the world are omitted. (b) Not separately computed in American national accounts.

As indicated in Table 2, the French tax structure is similar to those of Germany and the United Kingdom, and quite different from the United States, in the low degree of reliance on taxation of corporate profits. It differs from all three countries in the lightness of individual income taxation. Comparing indirect taxes to the total of income and profits taxation, France stands out: the ratio is nearly 3 to 1, far higher than in any of the other countries.

The general structure of the tax system, excluding social security taxes and benefits, is surely less progressive than in any of the other countries compared. It taxes consumption heavily, and lets incomes which are not spent on consumption get off lightly. Since it is the higher income groups which do most of the saving, they are the gainers. But this does not mean

---

[11]Cf. Tabatoni, *op. cit.,* pp. 308-309, and comment by Robert Liebaut, p. 330.

that the system is actually regressive. There are some income taxes, for which rates are progressive, and the tax on value added includes differential rates which bear more on luxury consumption. Furthermore, if social welfare payments and taxes are taken into consideration, it might be true that the French system as a whole could be considered relatively progressive.

It is impossible to make any convincing test, partly because the facts on income distribution in France are not known with any accuracy, but also because the real consequence of tax burdens is extremely difficult to disentangle from their intended incidence. Taxes on value added are in principle added to product prices, but they must in some cases work out to lower receipts to sellers: if the rates were increased, not all sellers would find it profitable to pass on the increases fully. Similarly, taxes on incomes and corporate profits are in principle borne by the one making the payment, but with imperfect markets they may sometimes be passed on in higher prices or wages than would otherwise have been charged.

Given the lack of information and the logical difficulties involved, calculations of the effects of the tax system on incomes cannot be regarded as more than interesting illustrations. But one such illustration, prepared by people associated with the Ministry of Finance, makes a good case against any conclusion that the system should be regarded as regressive. It suggests a fairly substantial net transfer from entrepreneurs and salaried cadres to all other groups, and most particularly to the inactive (retired and disabled) part of the population.[12]

Counting social security taxes in with all others, the present system achieves an amazingly high yield for a country in which people are individually good at escaping. "French tax collections amount to 44.2 percent of national income, the highest percentage in the world for a developed country."[13] That is undoubtedly helped by the fact that the tax on value added manages to be relatively invisible. It does not depend on individual willingness to declare earnings, and it is collected from producers rather than added explicitly to consumer prices as is usually done with American sales taxes.

Postwar tax reform has made it much easier to apply fiscal restraint to the economy when the government chooses to apply it. It has improved the rationality of the tax burden in the sense of making it more predictable and also in the sense of taxing all factors of production with lessened bias. It has enabled the government to encourage exports and investment relative to consumption. These are significant gains in making better management of the economy possible. They have come with a fairly systematic preference for light taxation of property incomes and heavy taxation of low income groups.

---

[12]Rivoli, *op. cit.*, pp. 78-84. The conclusion is supported by Wallace Peterson, *The Welfare State in France* (Lincoln, Nebraska: University of Nebraska Press, 1960).

[13]Norr and Kerlan, *op. cit.*, p. 67.

Growth and Prices 8

Between 1950 and 1960, with postwar reconstruction largely completed, gross national product per capita increased 41 percent. This was three times the rate of growth of production in France during the preceding century. It fell short of the pace of growth in Germany and Italy, as shown in Table 3 on page 94, but it still constituted what was perhaps the greatest improvement from prewar performance by any of the leading industrial countries.

Fast growth of output was accompanied by relatively rapid price increases. Although the actual rate of increase in prices slowed down somewhat in the course of the postwar period, the problem became increasingly troublesome in the 1960's because the country's choice in favor of more open international competition required better control of prices than it has as yet been able to manage.

Investment and Reallocation of Resources

The French growth rate has been greatly aided by a relatively high and stable ratio of investment to national product. Gross fixed capital formation averaged 20 percent of GNP for the whole period 1949–66, and stayed in the range between 18.7 and 21.8 in every year from 1957

TABLE 3.   Rates of Growth of Gross National Product per Capita, 1950–60 and 1960–66.

(Compound percentage rate of growth between terminal years)

	1950–1960	1960–1966
France	3.5	3.9
Germany	6.4	3.2
Italy	5.3	4.4
United Kingdom	2.2	2.3
United States	1.5	3.5
Combined total for all member countries of:		
OEEC	3.7	—
OECD	—	3.9

Note: The OEEC countries (Organization for European Economic Cooperation) included 17 European members; the OECD (Organization for Economic Cooperation and Development) also includes Canada, Japan, and the United States.
Sources: for 1950–60 OEEC, *General Statistics*, July, 1961, p. III, for 1960–66, OECD, *National Account Statistics*, 1957–66, Paris, 1968, p. 11. Revisions of French national accounts under discussion in late 1968, using a new base year, suggest that the indicated rate of growth for the 1960's is an underestimate and will be raised.

through 1966. By comparison, the same ratio for the United States for 1957–66 averaged 17 percent.[1]

Until the last few years, the French labor force was by far the most slowly growing of those in the main industrial countries. This permitted, for any given rate of growth of investment, a faster rate of growth of capital per worker than in other countries. Alain Cotta estimates that the capital-labor ratio more than doubled from 1949 to 1961.[2] As he points out, the higher birth rates of the early postwar years are now beginning to increase the labor force more rapidly, and this means that continuance of an unchanged ratio of investment to GNP will result in a slower rate of increase of capital per worker. The country's total output should rise faster, but output per man less rapidly.

Investment provided both new equipment for workers and rising demand for the economy as a whole. But its contribution to an explanation of the growth process may well have been outweighed by other factors. The most thorough attempt yet made to assess the quantitative significance of the main factors bearing on postwar European growth rates attributes only 26 percent of the growth of output in France, for the

---

[1]Ministère de l'Économie et des Finances, *Rapport sur les comptes de la nation de l'année 1966* (Paris: Imprimerie Nationale, 1967), pp. 490–91, and Organization for Economic Cooperation and Development, *National Accounts of OECD Countries, 1957–1966* (Paris: OECD, 1968), pp. 311, 316. The 1957–66 ratios are stated for data in constant 1958 prices.
[2]Alain Cotta, "La Croissance de l'économie française," 1945–1975," *Analyse et prévision,* July-August 1966, pp. 522, 553.

period 1950–62, to increased labor and capital inputs.[3] The other 74 percent of growth was attributed to improved efficiency in the use of productive factors, rather than increases in their quantity. Denison assigned 20 percent of total growth to "improved allocation of resources," meaning chiefly the shift of labor out of agriculture, and 16 percent to the residual category of general, unexplained improvements of efficiency not related to measurable changes in factor supply or allocation.

Denison concluded that France stood out among the nine European countries compared for the relative importance of improvements in management of resources. This, rather than increases in capital stock, is what "raises France from the position of a medium to a high growth rate country."[4] Still, the economy did not by any means catch up to the best techniques in use elsewhere. "Even in France the rate at which the gap was closing was rather slow in comparison to the apparent possibilities."[5]

Another suggestive study of European growth patterns, by Charles Kindleberger, emphasizes the reserve of poorly utilized labor in France at the beginning of the postwar period. In farming, older industries, and in many redundant trade and service occupations, people were earning low incomes doing things that could be handled better without them by reorganization of production and selling techniques. Once the pressure of rising demand and high investment created more valuable employment opportunities in new directions, they were ready to move. The movement helped supply the labor required by new industries, without raising costs so steeply as to erode the profits needed for continuing investment. But the very success of the process meant that the scope for continuing growth gradually narrowed, leading to higher wage costs, a squeeze on profits, and inflation. "Prices rose to the point where the balance of payments was threatened. Then in September, 1963 a stabilization plan of fiscal and monetary contraction was announced. . . . The spurt of very rapid growth was over."[6]

Kindleberger's conclusion that the earlier days of fast growth are definitely over, because the supply of previously under-utilized labor has been used up, seems unnecessarily pessimistic. The proportion of the labor force in agriculture is still three times as high as it is in the United States, and output per worker in retailing and other relatively backward sectors is still far below average. The opportunity cost of moving still

---

[3]Edward Denison and Jean-Pierre Poullier, *Why Growth Rates Differ* (Washington: The Brookings Institution, 1967), p. 307.

[4]*Ibid.*, p. 323.

[5]*Ibid.*, p. 340.

[6]*Europe's Postwar Growth* (Cambridge, Mass.: Harvard University Press, 1967), pp. 57-68, quote from pp. 65-66.

more workers from the backward to the more modern sectors may be rising, but the flow of new entrants to the labor force is increasing and could well offset any braking effect of this kind.

The actual performance of the economy from 1963 on has become more erratic. As shown in Chart 2 on page 97, the rate of growth of industrial production fell sharply in every other year from 1963, though it came back up again strongly each time. This pattern looks depressingly similar to the English stop-go experience through much of the postwar period, but there is at least one important difference. As shown in Chart 2, gross fixed investment in real terms kept rising rapidly. At the same time, unemployment increased persistently from 1963 through 1967. The situation seems to be that monetary restraints combined with continuing rapid increases in wage rates are putting increased pressure on firms to intensify efforts at labor saving. This should provide the basis for a faster rate of growth than before, if the basic hurdle of a price level seriously handicapping French producers' ability to compete against foreign firms can be overcome.[7]

A different kind of obstacle to rapid growth, a change in social preferences toward leisure rather than increased output, may well become more important over the next few years. The standard work week has been close to 47 hours through most of the postwar period. Overtime seemed to be generally desired by workers who were moving up into the range of incomes permitting them to catch up on modern consumer durables. But workers and the whole country seized immediately on the idea of extending vacations to four weeks when this was initiated by Renault in 1962, and labor representatives in the Economic and Social Council began to argue seriously for reduced weekly hours in discussions preceding the Fifth Plan. They were outvoted in the Council, but returned to the attack in the national labor negotiations of May, 1968. This time the government and the employers' associations agreed to the principle of shifting gradually to a standard 40-hour actual week in the course of the next several years. If this is followed through, it will mean several years in which a good share of annual gains in productivity will be taken in the form of increased leisure. That will make the growth rate lower, even though the reality may be a significant improvement in satisfaction of people's preferences.

Inflation

It is not going to be easy to satisfy any of the society's goals if prices keep on going up faster than in competing industrial countries. Inflation

---

[7] Cf. the relatively optimistic view of Denison and Poullier, *op. cit.*, p. 341.

CHART 2. Rates of growth of industrial production and fixed investment, 1960–1968

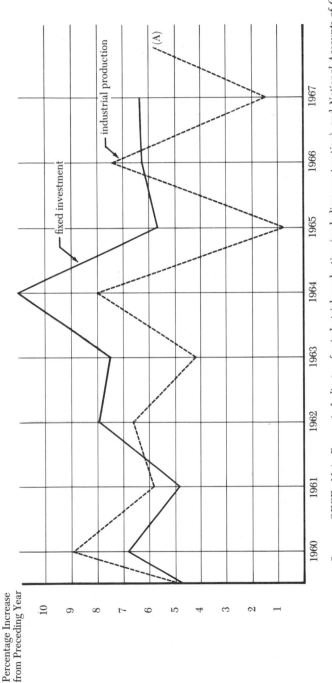

Sources: OECD, *Main Economic Indicators* for industrial production (excluding construction), and *National Accounts of OECD Countries, 1957–1966* (Paris: OECD, 1968), for investment data through 1966; *Rapport sur les comptes de la nation de l'annee 1967* (Paris: Imprimerie Nationale, 1968), for volume index of fixed investment for 1967.

Note (A): Industrial production for first quarter of 1968 compared to first quarter of 1967.

has become much less severe than it was in the early postwar years, as indicated in Chart 3 on page 99, but France still has too much of a tendency toward increasing prices to compete effectively for long periods at a fixed exchange rate.

The initial postwar inflation continued with only brief and partial periods of relief through 1951. It was a straightforward case of extreme budget deficits and rapid monetary expansion, complicated in 1950–51 by the effects of the Korean War on raw material prices. Government policy was directed overwhelmingly toward the objective of promoting investment and rapid reconstruction, with strictly secondary attention to price stabilization. The effects on import demand and export availability were naturally very adverse for the balance of payments, but American aid took care of this and allowed the fast pace of investment to continue. Still, public and external pressure to slow down the inflation became steadily stronger, and this became the main objective of the Pinay Government which took office in March, 1952.

Pinay was determined to stop the inflation, but tried to do it in a way that seemed to be a direct violation of economic principles. Either because of opposition from the coalition of government agencies which wanted to keep the investment program going in high gear, or because of a small-business habit of mind which considered easy credit to be vital, Pinay tried to combat inflation without monetary restriction. Instead, he revived price controls for producers, persuaded retail distributors to accept a standard voluntary markdown, and asked unions to stand still on wage claims. "On the surface, this may have seemed a naive policy, but to a certain extent it worked."[8]

Coming as it did at a time of incipient recession, but with prices and wages continuing to go up almost automatically, the Pinay program created a break in inflationary expectations and changed the whole climate. Hourly wage rates, which had been rising by an average of 6 percent per quarter in the two preceding years, slowed down to an average of less than 1 percent per quarter in 1952.[9] The cost of living index actually fell for several months, and did not again reach the level of March, 1952 until 1956. In the meantime, the option of continued monetary expansion worked to revive demand quickly and led to four years of exceptionally fast growth, with prices of basic industries under government control and with no inflation.[10]

---

[8]J.S.G. Wilson, *French Banking Structure and Credit Policy* (Cambridge, Mass.: Harvard University Press, 1957), p. 360.

[9]Marguerite Perrot, "Données Statistiques sur l'evolution des rémunérations salariales de 1938 à 1963," *Études et conjoncture*, August 1965, p. 23.

[10]John Sheahan, *Promotion and Control of Industry in Postwar France* (Cambridge, Mass.: Harvard University Press, 1963), pp. 212-214.

CHART 3. Annual Changes in Wholesale and Consumer Prices, 1949–1967

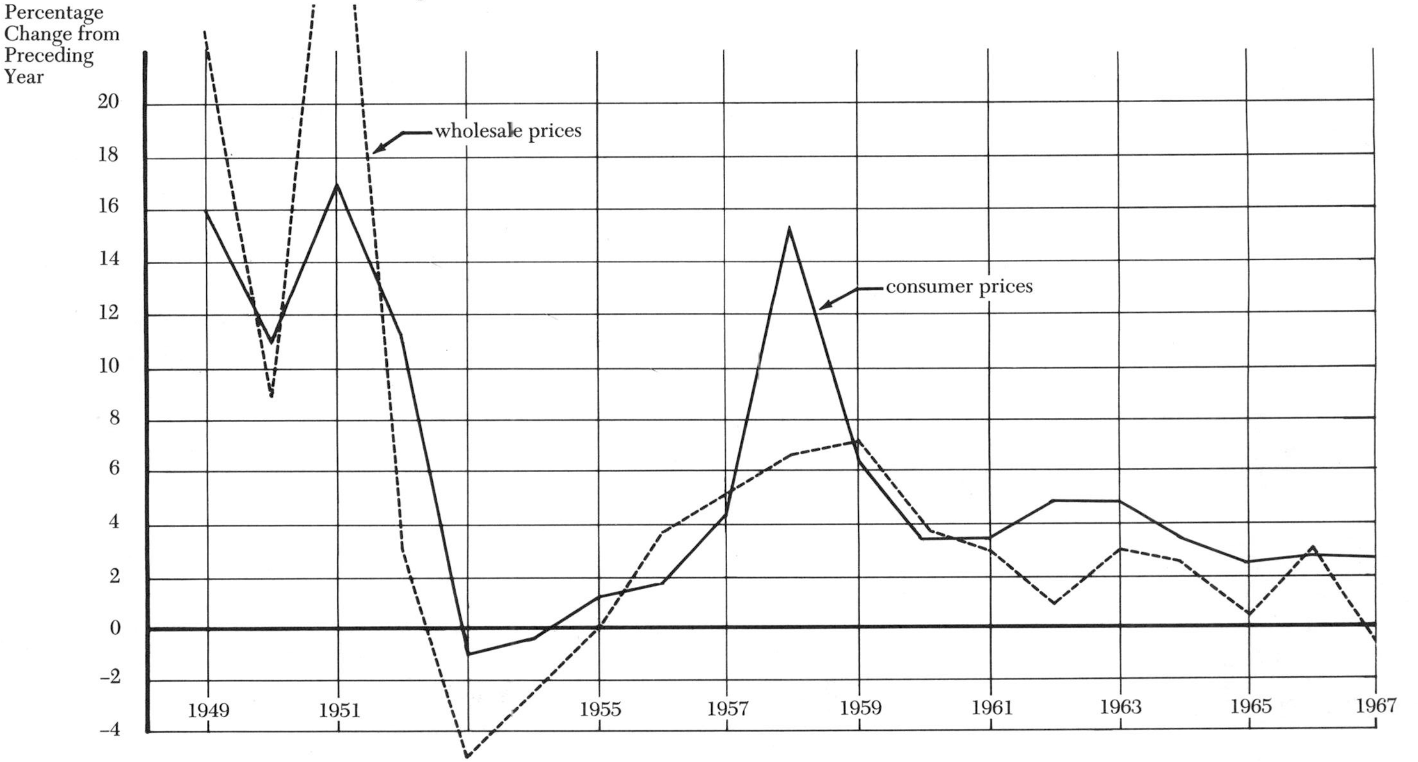

Percentage
Change from
Preceding
Year

wholesale prices

consumer prices

Sources: *Annuaire statistique de la France, 1966*, pp. 377, 389, 392, for 1949 to 1957; OECD, *Main Economic Indicators* for 1957 to 1967.

The period from early 1952 through 1956 marked a real turning point. At the beginning of the 1950's reconstruction had been accomplished, but the economy seemed to be running out of steam. An exceptionally acute observer writing in 1952–53, Herbert Luethy, was able to make a discouragingly convincing case for the belief that the economy was still bogged down by the same defensive atavism that had plagued France before the war.[11] Even the Planning Commission lowered its sights for the Second Plan in 1952, and tried to get the steel industry to hold back on possibly excessive investment. They were all wrong. The rate of growth overshot the plan, French industries raised investment with a new confidence that proved in most instances to be collectively self-justifying, prices stayed down, the balance of payments remained in better shape than at any time since the beginning of the 1930's, people moved into new industries from farming and other overcrowded occupations at surprising rates for a society long considered to be immobile, and economic expansion began to be generally accepted as a normal fact of life.

If the government had chosen monetary deflation in that period, the overly-conservative plan would have looked too ambitious, and the investment base that permitted effective participation in the Common Market after 1958 might never have been created. As a French author put it recently, the country was lucky to escape from "a brief but dangerous emphasis on monetary stability . . . the great difficulties with which Great Britain had been struggling for ten years would have been our lot if France had, in 1952–53, ceded to the temptations of 'stability'. . ."[12]

A gamble on ability to expand demand rapidly at low levels of unemployment always involves a risk of inflation. If an economy were highly competitive, the risk would be low as long as demand did not actually exceed supply possibilities. But French industries have no bias toward strong competition, and the government does not have any effective policies to promote it. Furthermore, in this period import controls kept to a minimum the role of foreign competition as a price-stabilizing pressure. In the circumstances, the option for expansion could have worked badly, and have been reversed quickly, if price controls had not served to some extent as a substitute for the absent force of competition.

Rapidly growing demand and production kept even with each other for about four years, but the balance was upset in the course of 1956. The war in Algeria led to greatly increased government spending and an intensified military draft, running into a situation of high investment demand and low unemployment. Given the fundamental mistake of the war itself, the situation called for tighter monetary policy and higher

---

[11]Translated as *France Against Herself* (New York: Frederick A. Praeger, Inc., 1955, and Meridian Books, 1957), esp. pp. 283-324.

[12]Jacques Guyard, *Le miracle français* (Paris: Éditions du Seuil, 1965), p. 26.

taxes to restrict consumption. The government chose instead to allow a large-scale balance-of-payments deficit as a means of dampening inflation. Nothing worked. External reserves ran out quickly. Despite nominal price regulations, the cost of living index went up 10 percent during 1957. And the civilian side of the government lost control to those in favor of stronger military action in Algeria. The Fourth Republic was swept out of existence in 1958.

Apart from marking the return of General de Gaulle and the start of the Fifth Republic, 1958 proved to be critical for economic policy. The country was still deeply involved in the war, its balance of payments and external reserve positions were extremely weak, and its price level had risen far out of line with those in competing countries. In this context, the possibility of implementing the French agreement to reduce trade barriers in the Common Market seemed completely blocked. The Planning Commission put its weight on the side of continued internal expansion and delayed reduction of restrictions on trade. The business community as a whole opposed any moves toward the Common Market in the immediate future. The new government ignored both of them.

A special commission was created to untangle the confusion. It was headed by an arch-conservative monetary theorist, Jacques Rueff, and an expansionist-minded "technocrat," Jean-Marcel Jeanneney. Between them, they put together a solution. The key step was to devalue the currency to make industrial exports competitive. France joined in the establishment of the Common Market and began to reduce its own trade barriers. A wide range of subsidies were reduced or eliminated. Cost-of-living escalators in wage contracts and in agricultural price support targets were made illegal. Taxes were increased and the budget deficit was reduced. But, once again, care was taken to keep the investment program going. Consumption was held back, but the money supply was allowed to go on rising in order to keep credit conditions from tightening, and fixed investment continued to increase.

The set of policies adopted at the end of 1958 successfully connected the French economy back to the outside competitive world. Protection remained important in the form of barriers around the Common Market itself, but the direction of policy marked a critical change from eighty years of insulation. Besides, it permitted another five years of fast growth with a favorable balance of payments, an achievement not to be disdained even though it was accompanied by renewed inflationary problems.

The rise in prices accompanying expansion from 1959 to 1963 was nothing like the all-out inflation of the early postwar years—the cost of living index went up 4.1 percent a year—but it had a more painful meaning in a more open trading system in which trade barriers were being progressively reduced. It threatened to cut the ground out from under industry's new-found export strength, and throw the balance of payments back into deficit.

One factor contributing to the greater difficulty with prices was that the money supply increased faster than it had in the mid-1950's. The annual rate of growth of the money supply in the 1952–56 period was 12 percent; from the end of 1959 to the end of 1963 it was 16 percent. The speed-up was related to two changes in underlying bank assets and lending. One of them was the new surplus in the balance of payments, which reached very high levels in 1961 and 1962. This became more important than total credit extensions to the public sector as a factor explaining the rise in assets of the banking system. Credit to the public sector did continue to increase, but at a rate not significantly different from that in the 1950's. Credit to the private sector, on the other hand, increased more than twice as rapidly as it had from 1953 through 1958.[13]

The balance of payments surplus after devaluation was to a considerable degree due to an inflow of investment from the United States. The inflow acted to increase the assets of the French banking system and thus to add to the rate of monetary expansion. The effect on prices might have been offset by allowing greater imports, but preference was given to the accumulation of gold. The French, or at least their President, concluded that the United States was causing inflation in France.

The problem with prices in this period was complicated by the adjustment to participation in the Common Market. After devaluation, French industrial prices were about on the same level as those in the other member countries, but food prices were relatively low. Reduction of trade barriers within the group acted to pull French food prices up toward the levels in the other countries, creating an inflationary symptom not directly related to domestic monetary conditions. An unusually good rise in agricultural production between 1958–59 and 1960–61 helped hold food prices down temporarily, but from then to 1963 production went nowhere and prices rose steeply. The food component of the cost-of-living index had been a stabilizing factor in the mid-1950's, but it led the general rise in the early 1960's. Further, by pulling up the general price index, food prices probably helped stimulate faster increases in wages and thus contributed to rising industrial costs.

By 1963, unit labor costs in manufacturing averaged 16 percent above their level in 1958, almost exactly offsetting the competitive advantage obtained by the devaluation.[14] Although the balance of payments remained strong, the government decided on the most restrictive aggregative policies adopted in the whole postwar period.

---

[13]Holger L. Engberg, "French Money and Capital Markets and Monetary Management," *The Bulletin* of the New York University Graduate School of Business Administration, Jan.-March, 1965, Table 8, p. 17.

[14]*National Institute Economic Review*, November, 1967, p. 68.

Deflation, Unemployment, and Present Policy Alternatives

In 1963 the Ministry of Finance prepared a "stabilization plan" overriding the official Fourth Plan. The rate of growth of the money supply was reduced to 8 percent a year from the end of 1963 to the end of 1966. Budget deficits had averaged six billion francs a year from 1960 through 1963; they were brought down to an average of one billion for 1964–66, including in 1965 that almost inconceivable rarity, an outright surplus. In addition, the government brought back into use the price control mechanism which it had suspended after the reforms of 1958.

The effect of these measures was mild but helpful from 1963 through 1965. The rates of increase of consumer and wholesale prices slowed down slightly, and the rate of fixed investment continued to rise. The policy seemed to be successful in eliminating excessive monetary expansion without checking the economy. But then, when retail price increases seemed to have levelled off at a rate slightly below 3 percent, and unemployment began to rise seriously, the government decided to keep right on with relatively intense restraint. In 1967, the rate of increase of industrial production fell sharply and unemployment rose to the highest level in the whole postwar period. That was still not a high level of unemployment by American standards, but far worse than the French have been used to. For the first time since the war, confidence of workers in their ability to find jobs, and of students in their chances of being employed in their fields of specialization, was seriously shaken.[15]

Whether or not continued deflation through 1967 served any positive function is a tantalizing question. It was clearly harmful for growth and employment. It did not, after 1965, accomplish anything further to slow down the rates of increase of prices or wages. It failed to come to grips with the non-monetary factors acting to raise costs after excess demand was eliminated. But there was still a real problem to be met. Despite the restraint on domestic demand, the current account surplus in the balance of payments practically disappeared in 1966 and 1967, and export prices of manufactured goods increased relative to those of the country's closest competitors. From 1963 to 1967, prices of French manufacturing exports increased 8 percent, those of West Germany rose 4 percent, and those of Italy actually decreased 1 percent.[16] As shown in Table 4, these changes in relative prices corresponded closely to changes in market shares for industrial exports: the French share slipped progressively, while those of Germany and especially of Italy increased.

---

[15]The government does not publish unemployment figures as a percentage of the labor force. The index usually taken as a guide is the number of registered "unsatisfied demands for jobs." For the first quarter of 1968, this totalled 270,000. From past census benchmarks, this is taken to indicate an actual level of about half a million involuntarily unemployed, which corresponds to about 2.5 percent of the labor force.

[16]*National Institute Economic Review*, August, 1968, p. 69.

TABLE 4. Relative Shares of Exports of Manufactured Goods by France and Other Industrial Countries, 1960–1967.

Percentages of exports of manufactures by 11 countries[a]

	France	Germany	Italy	Japan	United Kingdom	United States
1960	9.7	19.3	5.1	6.9	16.3	21.6
1965	8.8	19.2	6.8	9.4	13.5	20.5
1966	8.6	19.5	6.9	9.8	12.9	20.2
1967	8.5	19.7	7.0	9.8	11.9	20.5

Source: *National Institute Economic Review*, August, 1968, Table 23, p. 69.
Note (a): The other countries included in the total used to calculate market shares were Belgium-Luxemburg, Canada, The Netherlands, Sweden, and Switzerland.

Widening antagonism to continued deflation as a solution induced the government to adopt a moderately more expansionary policy in early 1968, but then led to the general explosion of May before this change had much effect. Major wage concessions in the *Grenelle Accords* at the end of May added to the existing difficulty with prices. Costs were suddenly raised for both industries and government, leading to some immediate price increases and to a jump in the government's operating expenditures. Although some taxes were raised as well, the net effect on both aggregate demand and costs of production have driven the economy into a most difficult corner.

The government's initial response was to create temporary export subsidies, and to impose quotas, for the remainder of 1968, on imports of automobiles, steel, and some textile products. But concern over inflation and possible devaluation continued to show up in a massive flight of capital, and the government then had to turn back toward reduction of demand as the price of avoiding devaluation. In the circumstances, devaluation would seem to be a better choice, in the sense that it would have allowed both more expansionary domestic policies and the avoidance of selective restraints on trade and travel. It could conceivably have restored the competitive position achieved in 1958 and gradually lost in the following years.

Why does France seem to have so much more difficulty coping with inflation than Germany or Italy do? It is not simply a question of the rate of increase of wages: in the 1960's, they have been going up faster in Germany and Italy than in France. It may at times be a matter of excessively rapid monetary expansion, as it was in 1957–58 and again in the early 1960's. But even after the stabilization plan of 1963 slowed down monetary expansion, reduced government deficits, and raised unemployment, it seemed to run into a lower limit for price and wage increases that it could not further reduce. There is little question that intense deflationary measures could stop them by driving the economy into a really severe depression, but again it should be noted that Germany and Italy do not seem to need any such drastic remedy. Why should the French?

The underlying problem seems to be that the economy is still not sufficiently flexible in its response to market pressures. If producers were highly competitive, quick to respond to changing preferences, and quick to take advantage of new ways to reduce costs, inflation would be much less troublesome. It could still be caused by excessive monetary expansion, but it could be cured by monetary measures without persistently rising unemployment. France has been biased toward rising prices because it takes the productive system longer than it should to correct disequilibria. In comparison to the prewar economy, the situation has been enormously improved. But it still does not seem to have improved enough to allow France to stay even with Germany and Italy.

One possible answer to the present situation might be to keep the economy perpetually subject to mild deflation. That is not a very good answer, because it would condemn French industry to third-rate status. The country may have been lucky that its students and workers exploded in 1968, refusing to accept the way things were going. Another path might be to combine steady competitive pressure from abroad with collectively negotiated compromises on income flows, calculated to keep costs and prices down at levels of full employment. All groups in the society would have to agree to accept slower increases in money incomes than they are now apparently able to obtain, in return for higher rates of growth of real income than the economy can provide if it has to accept continuing unemployment.

The scheme for such a solution worked out in connection with the Fifth Plan has been completely ignored in practice. That may be inevitable while labor distrusts both business and the government as much as it still seems to, business keeps giving organized labor further reasons for profound antagonism, and the government's best technocrats still approach such questions with a preference for imposing solutions rather than a framework for joint bargaining. The path seems too hard to follow at present. As long as that is so, the choice is reduced to recurrent devaluation, to deflation and higher unemployment, or to retreat from open competition in international trade and thereby from the main pressures toward improving efficiency. Of these, devaluation is by far the best; it is the one most favorable for continued improvement of flexibility, providing the hope of eventually full-fledged ability to compete openly at high rates of growth.

The problem is neither a case of unlucky accident with respect to particular policies, nor one of inevitable bias beyond hope of correction.

It involves rather the whole postwar struggle to modernize the economy, to introduce the pressures of international competition, to provide pro motional assistance to help French firms catch up with more efficient techniques, to remove artificial barriers to market forces within the economy, and to open wider opportunities for capable people to participate in decision making.

Goals and Performance 9

The more consciously directed economy of the postwar period worked
far better than the prewar system with respect to improvement of efficiency and growth, if not as successfully as might be wished with respect
to price stability. Compared to other capitalist countries with less controlled economies, the postwar growth record is still inferior to the best
achieved elsewhere, but it has moved up from definitely sub-par to a
decent average. The prewar brand of capitalism in France, in which the
private sector was neither dynamic nor very competitive, and the government interfered a lot but without much sense of direction, combined
a collection of defects which would never have permitted the rates of
growth achieved since the war. The postwar changes in policy both
forced the private sector to face more external competition and changed
the government's role to one supporting modernization. Intervention was
probably increased, but what mattered was that it was given more coherence and better direction. That made for a much better form of capitalism than France had before.

Efficiency and growth are not the only relevant measures of success.
Criteria of performance should also include such objectives as personal
security, freedom of choice, equality, and open access to opportunity.
That need not exhaust the list, but any economy that serves all of these

goals well is a good one. The postwar French economy has not served them all equally well, by any means.

Personal Security

The fact that the prewar system performed poorly in terms of efficiency was not an indication that the business community and the government were helpless or irrational, but rather that they placed, if one may judge from their choices, a higher value on maintenance of familiar forms of social and economic equilibrium. They apparently wished to provide security more than they wished to promote growth. The form of capitalism they protected, with its cartels, import restrictions, and legal impediments to change, served its purpose relatively well for a long time. It broke down and failed to serve that purpose in the 1930's, when radical changes in policy were needed to restore employment opportunities, to rescue the farm and business sectors from collective bankruptcy, and to ease the state of warfare between labor and business.

The same approach in other spheres of social choice, the same emphasis on security and reliance on past methods, failed even more bleakly in the face of direct military challenge to the nation, first by lack of preparation for it in the second half of the 1930's, and then by collapse in action. Disaster drove home the conclusion that security is not ensured by resisting change, by trying to repeat the past, but by continuously trying to find ways to do things better. In the economic system, that meant modernization and growth, to ensure that France could keep up with outside competition and to provide the country with a strong base for meeting all its material objectives. It was not so much that the French changed fundamental goals, as that the prewar system broke down and failed to meet them. This made it easier for those people who wanted to change the systems to lead the way in new directions during the early postwar years.

Has the postwar system worked better in terms of provision of security? In a strictly economic sense, the answer is surely yes. The country's social welfare programs, with good coverage for medical care and retirement, special benefits for families with many children, and insurance for accidents and unemployment, give a high degree of personal protection to nearly everyone. These programs are infinitely superior to anything provided in prewar France, and close to the best achieved in any country so far.

The security provided by the social welfare programs was powerfully supported, until the last few years, by nearly continuous full employment and rising markets. Both workers and business could count on regular earnings if they made any serious effort to respond to market preferences, because aggregate demand was kept persistently close to the country's productive capacity. That is a crucial aspect of security in any modern economy. France has scored high in this respect, far higher than prewar and about as well as the best industrial economies in the postwar period.

Freedom of Choice

The scope for individual choice in economic matters has unquestionably been improved for consumers and for workers. The consumer can buy with little or no restriction the products of all the member countries of the Common Market, and can also buy from the outside world with lower tariffs and fewer direct restrictions than before the war. Not only that, he has a much more diversified, innovating, and cost-conscious set of domestic producers to choose among than he ever had before.

Workers, both in the industrial sector and in farming, have gained something vital: a chance to move freely in a wide variety of directions. This change was a product of fast economic growth and high demand for labor, not necessarily related to the multiple forms of direct control being practiced by the government. But insofar as planning and promotional intervention had the effect of aiding the growth process, they also helped increase occupational freedom.

For the firm, the postwar era has involved a mixture of increasing intervention, new opportunities, and increased competition from the outside. The reductions of trade barriers probably were more immediately important than everything else put together. High costs had always served as a justification for high prices; they became instead a threat of possible disaster. Reliance on domestic suppliers for inputs had been nearly inescapable; it became a matter of choice, with an improvement of possible qualities and costs for the firms producing end products.

It must remain a matter of doubt as to whether the net effect on the freedom of firms to invest and produce in ways they might prefer has increased or decreased. Before the war, the firm had to satisfy an investment banker to get outside funds, or had to satisfy itself with the rate of activity that could be financed from inside sources. After the war, the situation was not greatly changed for the majority of the smaller companies, but the larger firms seeking substantial amounts of external finance had to satisfy the Planning Department. Given approval for projects connected with modernization, the more expansionary companies probably could get credit for investment more easily than ever before. The new system favored those firms most interested in expansion and large scale, the corporation as against the family-owned concern, and probably the producer-goods industries as against those providing goods to consumers. It probably did not cripple those it least favored. In fact, many of the consumer goods industries outpaced some of those given particular help.

Those observers who conclude that firms do fairly much what they themselves choose, despite the formal planning apparatus, are much closer to the truth than those who see a rigid process of central determination.

This does not mean that what the firms choose after the planning confrontations is necessarily what they would have chosen in its absence. "Planning" in the sense actually practiced is chiefly a process of widening the scope of information available to all sides, emphasizing the possibilities of collective expansion, and exploring the range of assistance the government can offer. There must be many firms which ignore the whole thing in reaching their decisions. There must also be many which find new possibilities for expansion, market openings of which they were not fully aware, a means to put pressure on their own suppliers or customers, or simply a marginal consideration which tilts the balance among alternatives that they were already considering on their own. It would be surprising if the operation did not change some people's minds on what to do, but it hardly amounts to any system of compulsion limiting their freedom.

Equity

Postwar policies suggest that questions of equity have been considered secondary to the goal of industrial modernization. Two powerful techniques have somewhat offset each other: social welfare expenditures adopted at the start of the postwar period have done a great deal to decrease inequality, especially by protection of the retired and disabled, but the tax structure has been shaped to place burdens more on consumers and workers as against property incomes. This is surely not because of any preference for maintenance of inequality. In a number of ways, such as the differential rates for luxury goods used in the tax on value added, and the progressive rates of the income tax (kept in a very minor role within the whole structure), efforts have been made to direct the burden toward people in a better position to support it.

The main differentiation running through tax policy is not between richer people and poorer, but between forms of income which go toward investment and those which go toward consumption. Every effort is made to protect the flow of income into investment, and to place the main tax burden in ways that will restrain consumption. As compared to the American or the English tax systems, this has the general effect of easing taxes on owners of productive property and placing them more on workers and the inactive population. That is, the French structure places the goals of efficiency and growth higher relative to the goal of equity.

The same general option in favor of efficiency when it seems to conflict with equity, and investment as against consumption, shows up emphatically in labor relations. Union intervention in work practices and in the establishment of pay differentials is held to a strict minimum. The result leaves employers greater freedom to take measures favorable for efficiency than they have in most other industrial countries, and also leaves them relatively free to exploit a dominant position.

When the government created an obligatory profit-sharing scheme in 1967, intended to reduce conflict between labor and business, it was remarkably careful to avoid any effect that might have redirected income from firms to workers: the costs are covered by the government as long as firms are willing to use such subsidies for new investment.

The structure of the scheme for profit sharing is particularly suggestive as to policy preferences. The subsidies envisaged are not designed to protect the profits of owners; they are designed to protect the flow of financing available for investment by the firm. The objective is to support *the firm* considered as an independent institution. Similarly, many of the "pro-business" options in the plans favor investment without any distinction between privately owned and government owned companies. The incidental effect is to increase the wealth of property owners, when the firms given aid are privately owned. But one might almost deduce that policies working this way were devised to minimize the effect on profit, treating it as if it were a tax to be accepted only insofar as it is directly related to investment.

Access to New Opportunities

The growth and gradual diversification of the economy in the postwar period have opened up much greater possibilities for entry of new firms, as well as greater professional opportunities for the rising proportion of young people able to go through the educational system. At the same time, many of the characteristics of the society that have always acted to reserve favored positions for better placed groups have maintained great strength.

The society is surely more open than it was before the war, but not extraordinarily flexible even now. That might be explained as a consequence of social preferences for predictable relationships. "Certain values constitute the prevailing patterns—the values of harmony, security, and independence . . . the primacy given to rational well-ordered mastery of the environment. Frenchmen do not dislike change; they dislike disorder, conflict, everything that may bring uncontrolled relationships . . . ."[1] That explanation is highly suggestive, but perhaps not the whole story. That substantial fraction of the population constituted by urban workers is almost totally unrepresented in the political process and has had little say in shaping educational institutions. Workers may not fully share the preference for stabilized social relationships, but what they prefer is not allowed to matter much.

The speed of economic growth has multiplied openings and increased requirements for capable people to handle more responsibilities within

---

[1] Michel Crozier, *The Bureaucratic Phenomenon* (Chicago: University of Chicago Press, 1964), p. 226.

both business and government. Higher incomes and renewed population growth simultaneously led to rapidly increasing entries into the educational system. The two forces could have been wedded to provide both personal opportunities and improving solutions to the needs of a modernizing economic system. To some extent, this did happen. But it happened too slowly, in the sense that both the economy and the growing numbers of people going through the educational system were partially blocked. Neither governmental administrative agencies nor private company management have tried greatly to decentralize decisions and widen the range of responsibility. They continue to act as if the society could not provide more than a few key leaders who had to manage everything, despite a situation requiring greater flexibility and quicker response to new technological opportunities. The French did better than before on all the old basic industries—steel, automobiles, heavy electrical equipment—but woke up belatedly to discover from an influx of American subsidiaries that they were distinctly behind in newer fields closely related to scientific progress.

Those concerned with education have tried a succession of reforms, and have managed miraculously to cope with rapidly expanding numbers under the handicap of severely restricted financing, but they never really broke through to correct the motivational patterns and economic obstacles that acted to screen out the great majority of children from farm or labor families. Class discrimination in education remained glaringly apparent, wasting much of the society's potential capacities. Further, the universities remained a second-best form of higher education, handling many more people but preparing them in relatively rigid ways for specific professions, while the key openings remained reserved for the small fraction going through the *grandes écoles*. The structure reenforced the general propensity in both business and government toward centralized direction from the top downward, impeded flexibility, and still acts to give the economy somewhat the flavor of that of an underdeveloped country.

Intervention and Performance

The economy is much more progressive than it used to be, but less open and flexible than it could be. The imperfections are sometimes blamed on excessive intervention by the government. Sometimes they should be: there are too many rules and special favors. Well-established firms get too many advantages relative to new companies. But as a general proposition the idea that intervention has seriously held back the economy is surely wrong. Most of the postwar economic policies have been designed, and have worked, to give the economy greater dynamism than it would have had in their absence. The society has many built-in handicaps, derived from attitudes and customs more appropriate to a stagnant, aristocratic system. The economic policies of the government have partially offset these handicaps, creating pressures for change and better adaptation to the modern world.

Cultural and intellectual traditions in France give great value to "rational, well-ordered mastery of the environment . . ." The French dislike "everything that may bring uncontrolled relationships."[2] Americans usually favor holding government intervention to a minimum unless a strong case can be made for it in exceptional circumstances; the French on the contrary prefer conscious control unless its costs are so high as to make a strong case against it in exceptional circumstances. Either economic planning or some alternative institutional system that permits conscious guidance of the economy may be considered to be among the *goals* of the society, valued for their own sake.

Neither a preference for conscious control nor the opposite position can be condemned as valid goals. The operation of the French economy in the prewar period can be criticized, and should be, for paying a very high price in lost opportunities because of a confusion between conscious control and the quite different question of the use of market froces to achieve desired goals. The distrust of market forces led to policies of import restriction, elaborate internal controls by the government, and extensive use of monopolistic arrangements by private groups. But none of these measures constituted any positive direction of choices toward explicitly chosen goals. All this approach accomplished was to impede change and protect privilege.

Postwar policy has been markedly better, in that objectives have been formulated more explicitly and the costs of alternatives compared more systematically. But beyond that it has included a genuine, if still erratic, recognition that market forces can be used to implement consciously selected programs. Instead of relying on legal restrictions to force through desired reorganization in the steel industry in the early postwar years, the government offered to reduce costs of investment and simultaneously lowered import protection so that firms would be forced to act. Instead of waiting for long-run structural changes to make French industry competitive in export markets, the exchange rate was used in 1958 to make exporting more profitable. Ancient complaints about the bias of companies toward small scale were backed up by revision of taxes discriminating against large companies, by reduction of import barriers, and by removal of retail price maintenance. It is true that all these policies have gone back and forth in inconsistent ways, but they may still be seen as part of a growing understanding that market forces are neither unpredictable nor inherently contrary to conscious pursuit of specified social goals.

---

[2]*Ibid*; cf. the explanation by Pierre Massé of the fundamental meaning of French economic planning, quoted on p. 71.

Economic policy has combined planning with greater use of market forces in the postwar period and the economy has performed better than it ever did before. The achievement has not been extraordinary in comparison to other capitalist countries, because nearly all of them have been doing better too. This is partly because they have accepted more fully the need to devise new answers to meet specific difficulties rather than to wait for automatic corrective processes that may or may not occur. In a sense, most of the capitalist countries have gone in the direction that the French have always preferred, making deliberate decisions to change the operation of their economies to conform more closely with social preferences. The gains have not depended on replacing market forces with centralized direction, but on altering incentives so that decentralized decisions are taken in ways consistent with social goals. At the same time, French policy has been changing away from the morbid distrust of market forces that marked prewar intervention, and in the process has truly been achieving a higher degree of rational control.

Index

Agriculture:
    exports and imports, 3, 9-10, 12-15
    labor force, 3, 10, 12, 16, 18, 95
    planning, 12-14, 19
    prices, market supports, 3, 10, 12-19,
        101, 102
    social security for farm families, 17,
        61-62
    structure of production and incomes,
        9-10, 12-14, 17-19, 77, 78
    (see also Meat, Sugar beets, Wheat,
        Wine)
Aluminum industry, 23, 33
American aid (Marshall Plan), 72, 98
Amiens, Charter of, 39
Anarchists, 38-39
Ardagh, John, 67, 88
Aron, Raymond, 54
Automobile industry, 25, 28-31, 104, 112
Aviation industry, 26, 28

Balance of payments, 98, 100-104
Banks, 25, 26, 78, 83-85
Bauchet, Pierre, 27, 74
Baum, Samuel, 22
Bénard, Jean, 78
Birth rate, 4, 60
Bloch-Lainé, François, 35, 51
Blum, Léon, 5, 25, 40
Bourdieu, Pierre, 67
Bright, Arthur A., Jr., 23
Business:
    attitudes, motivation and size, 2, 4,
        21-25, 33
    organized groups, 2, 44, 74
    popular support, 6
    (see also Centralization of decision
        making, Competition, Concen-
        tration, Family firms)

Caisse Nationale des Dépôts et Consigna-
    tions, 84-85
Capitalism, French version, 1-2, 25, 107-
    108, 112-13

Carey, James B., 38
Cartels (see Business, Competition)
Cazes, Bernard, 65, 74
Centralization of decision making:
    in firms, 50-52
    in labor negotiations, 40, 44, 54-55
    national tradition, 3, 71, 105, 112
    relationship to educational system, 66-
        68, 106, 112
Chemical industry, 23, 26
Citroën, 28-29, 52
Clough, Shepard B., 3
Club Jean Moulin, 54
Coal industry, 26, 27, 43, 72
Common Market (see European Economic
    Community)
Communist Party, communism, 6, 38, 42
Competition:
    imports, 3, 9-11, 32, 104, 109
    industrial, 23, 25, 28, 36, 52
    national policy, 2, 25, 32, 100, 101
    (see also Mergers, Protective policies)
Concentration, size of firms, 31-34, 72, 89-
    90
Confédération française démocratique du
    travail (CFDT), 42, 43, 53-54, 77
Confédération française des travailleurs
    chrétiens (CFTC), 39, 42
Confédération générale du travail (CGT),
    38-41, 53-54
Conseil national du patronat français
    (CNPF), 44
Cotta, Alain, 94
Crédit National, 84-85
Crozier, Michel, 66, 111

de Gaulle, Charles, 6, 52, 101
de Ghellinck, Guy, 24
Denison, Edward F., 12, 18, 95, 96
Denton, Geoffrey, 76
Despax, Michel, 44
Devaluation (see Exchange rate)
Devaux, A., 48
D'Iribarne, Alain, 31

115

Doctors, fees and supply, 62-63
Dubergé, Jean, 88

Economic and Social Council, 79-80, 96
Eckstein, Otto, 89
Edding, F., 68
Education, 65-69, 111-12
Ehrmann, Henry W., 25, 39, 40, 44
Eide, K., 68
Electric power and gas, the EDF, 25, 26,
      27, 72-73
Employment, 4, 48, 53, 77, 81, 103-105,
      108-109
Engberg, Holger L., 84, 85, 86, 102
Ensemble, Julien (pseudonym), 80
European Economic Community (Com-
      mon Market), 15-19, 31, 32, 89, 101-
      102
Exchange rate:
      devaluation of 1958, 32, 48, 78, 101-
            102
      devaluations of 1920's and 1936, 5
      strains with fixed rate since 1958, 64-
            65, 98, 104-105
Exports:
      and prices, 65, 101-104
      agricultural, 13-15
      industrial, 4, 24, 28-29, 32-33, 64-65,
            103-104, *table* 94
      subsidies, 11, 13, 15-16
      tax relief, 88-89

Family allowances, 58-60
Family firms, 24-25, 29, 35, 51
*Fédération nationale des syndicats d'exploi-
      tants agricoles* (FNSEA), 14
Fein, Rashi, 62
Force Ouvrière (CGT-FO), 42
Foreign investment in France, 34, 52, 102,
      112
Forsyth, Murray, 76

Galbraith, J. K., 51
Gaullier, Jean-Pierre, 84
Gilpin, Robert, 35, 66
Goals and attitudes:
      change, modernization, 4, 6, 11
      conscious control of economy, 2-3,
            72, 113
      freedom of choice, opportunity, 66-
            68, 109-12
      multiplicity of objectives, 107
      personal security, 57-58, 107-109
      (*see also* Business, Centralization of
            decision making, Income distri-
            bution)
Government-owned corporations, 6, 25-29,
      44, 54, 84-85, 90

Government regulation, direct controls:
      credit allocation, 85-87
      industry, 21-22, 98
      labor markets, 40-41, 45-46, 51-55
      medical fees, 61
      prices, 98, 103
      relationships to efficiency and growth,
            107, 112-13
      (*see also* Planning, Protective policies)
Grandjeat, Pierre, 60, 61, 62
Grenelle Accords (May, 1968), 46, 96, 104
Growth rate and national income, 3-5, 18,
      76-77, 80, 85, 93-105, 107 *chart*
      97, *table* 94
Gruson, Claude, 78
Guyard, Jacques, 100

Hackett, John and Anne-Marie, 74, 79
Hamilton, Richard F., 37
Hochard, J., 59
Hohenberg, Paul M., 23
Hours of work, 5, 40-41, 64, 96
Housing, 30, 65, 78, 84
Houssiaux, Jacques, 32, 34

Imports:
      and inflation, 65, 98, 100, 102
      food, 3, 9-10, 12, 15
      industrial products, 30, 32, 75, 104
      see also Protective policies
Incentives and efficiency, 2, 21-26, 57,
      64-65
Income distribution, 49-50, 58-59, 63, 76-
      77, 90-91, 110-11
Incomes policy (price stabilization), 76-77,
      105
Industry:
      exports and imports, 3, 30, 32-33,
            103-104
      production, 3-4, 22
      structure, 22-24, 30-34, 36, 105, 109
      (*see also* specific industries)
Inflation (*see* Prices)
Insurance, medical, 17, 59-63
Investment:
      family firms, 24
      government corporations, 26-29, 72-
            73
      level and growth, 65-66, 93-94, *chart*
            97
      planning, 29-30, 72-77, 84-85, 109
      tax incentives, 53, 88-89, 110-11
      (*see also* Foreign investment, Social
            investment)

Jeanneney, Marcel, 101
Jeunesse Agricole Chrétienne (JAC), 14
Jouhaux, Léon, 39

Kerlan, Pierre, 89, 91
Kindleberger, Charles P., 3, 24, 75, 95

Labor:
    bargaining practices, 28, 40-41, 43-46
    organization, 38-43
    political position, attitudes, 6-7, 37-
      39, 54-55, 111
    supply, sector allocation, 3-4, 10, 18,
      22, 94-97, 109
    (*see also* Employment, Hours of work,
      Strikes, Wages)
Le Brun, Pierre, 50, 80
Liebaut, Robert, 90
Lorwin, Val R., 6, 39
Leuthy, Herbert, 25, 100

Maclennan, Malcolm, 76
Mandy, P. L., 24
Massé, Pierre, 71, 77, 78
Matignon Agreements, 40, 46, 54
Meat and livestock, 13, 15, 19
Medical insurance, 17, 58-63
Méline Tariff, 10
Mergers, 33-34
Moitrier, Jean, 58
Monetary policy and techniques:
    inflation, 76, 85, 100-105
    selective credit, 30, 78, 85-87
    techniques of control, 83-86
    see also Banks
Monnet, Jean, 72, 81
Morisot, Michel, 66, 67
Myon, J., 44

National Credit Council, 85
Nationalization (*see* Government-owned
    corporations)
Norr, Martin, 89, 91

Ogrel, Herbert, 45, 50
Ousset, Jean, 13

Parliamentary control and democratic
    procedures, 54-55, 79-81
Participation by workers in management,
    50-52, 54
Passeron, Jean-Claude, 67
Perrot, Marguerite, 46, 50, 98
Peterson, Wallace C., 58, 64, 91
Peugeot, 28-29
Pinay, Antoine, 48, 86, 98
Planning:
    agriculture, 11-15, 18-19
    growth rate, 100, 103, 113
    ideology, 3, 21-22, 71-72, 75
    implementation, 29-30, 72-75, 77-79,
      84-87, 89-90

    industrial, 26, 29-31, 33, 35, 109-10
    introduction of, 1, 6, 25, 71-72
    social, 65-66, 77-78
    (*see also* Incomes policy, Investment,
      Parliamentary control)
Popular Front, 5, 11, 40, 71-72
Population, 3-4, 58-60
Poujade, Pierre, 88
Poullier, Jean-Pierre, 12, 95, 96
Prices:
    flexibility of economy, 100, 104-106
    negotiated stabilization in 1952, 48,
      86, 98
    prewar inflations, 5
    rates of increase, 98-103, *chart* 99
    relative to other countries, 32, 96-
      105
    social security taxes, 64-65
    stabilization plan of 1963, 76-77, 95
    (*see also* Agriculture, Exchange rate,
      Government regulation, In-
      comes policy)
Productivity, 27, 31, 94-96
Profits:
    attitudes toward, 1-2
    incomes policy, 77
    level, 95
    sharing with workers, 51-53, 111
    taxation, 89-90
Protective policies:
    agriculture, 3, 9-11, 15-16
    industry, 25, 32, 100
    revisions beginning in 1958, 101, 104,
      109
    (*see also* Competition, Goals, Gov-
      ernment regulation)
Public enterprise (*see* Government-owned
    corporations)

Radio and television (ORTF), 54
Railroad system (SNCF), 18, 26, 27, 43, 73
Renault, 25, 26, 28-29, 44-45
Research, 17, 22-23, 33, 35-36, 65, 112
Retail trade, 32, 88, 95, 98
Reynaud, Jean-Daniel, 40, 42, 44
Rivoli, Jean (pseudonym), 88, 91
Rosen, Henry, 61
Ross, Arthur M., 50
Rueff, Jacques, 101

SAFER, 17
Salem, Daniel, 10
Sawyer, John E., 24
Scale of plants, 31, 33-34, 72 (*see also*
    Concentration)
Schuman Plan (Coal-Steel Community),
    30, 32

Servan-Schreiber, Jean-Jacques, 35
Sheahan, John, 28, 32, 77, 98
Shonfield, Andrew, 75, 79, 84, 85
Simca, 28
Social investment, 65-69, 76-78, 80
Social security, 17, 53, 57-69, 90-91, 108, 110, *table* 59
Social stratification, 66-69, 111-12
Socialist Party, 5, 11
Steel industry, 23, 30, 72-73, 75, 89, 104, 112
Strikes:
    Ideology and types, 6, 38, 43-44
    May, 1963, 40
    May, 1968, 7, 46, 52-55, 63, 96, 104-105
Sturmthal, Adolf, 41
Subsidies:
    exports, 15-16
    government corporations, 27
    investment, 73, 85-86, 109, 111, 113
    transportation, 18
Sugar beet production and marketing, 2, 12-13, 18
Svennilson, Ingvar, 24

Syndicalism, 38-39, 54
Tabatoni, Pierre, 88, 89, 90
Tariffs (*see* Protective policies)
Taxes:
    administration and collection, 25, 88, 91
    agriculture, 13
    distribution of income, 38, 58-59, 83, 90-91, 110-11
    private tax systems, 2, 32
    social security, 55, 64, 65
    special incentives, 33, 52-53, 83, 87-89
    structure, 87-91, *table* 90
Technological change, 23-24, 34-36
Telephone service, 26, 27
Textile industry, 2, 23, 24, 32, 86, 104
Tracy, Michael, 10, 12, 13, 15

Wages, 37, 46-50, *chart* 47
Weber, A.D., 34
Wheat, 10-11, 15-16, 19
Wilson, J.S.G., 84, 98
Wine, 10-12, 14
Wright, Gordon, 10, 11, 14